THE FAITH OF CATHOLICS

The Faith of Catholics

by
Richard Chilson, C.S.P.

PAULIST PRESS
New York / Paramus / Toronto

ACKNOWLEDGMENT

Excerpts from the English translations of the Order of Mass, Rite of Baptism for Children, Rite of Marriage, Rites of Funerals, and Rites for Holy Week, copyright © 1969, 1970, International Committee on English in the Liturgy, Inc. All rights reserved.

Library of Congress
Catalog Card Number: 72-81229

Published by Paulist Press
Editorial Office: 1865 Broadway, N.Y., N.Y., 10023
Business Office: 400 Sette Drive, Paramus, N.J. 07652

Printed and bound in the
United States of America

Contents

Introduction: The Restless Animal   1

Part I

The Stories of Christianity

1. The Stories of the Israelites   9
2. The Stories of Jesus   19
3. From Experience to Expression   28

Part II

The Dogmas of Christianity

4. To the Depths of Meaning   35
5. The Foundations of Christology   42

Part III

The Rituals of Christianity

6. The Drama of Worshsip   51
7. Sacraments of Initiation—Baptism and Confirmation   60
8. Sacrament of Christian Nourishment and Growth—Eucharist   74

Part IV

The Ethics of Christianity

9. The Wander and Mystery of Man 87
10. The Christian's Own Story 96

Part V

The Rituals of Christianity (continued)

11. Sacraments of Healing—Reconciliation and Anointing 115
12. Sacraments of Christian Witness—Marriage and Priesthood 124

Part VI

The Social Institutions of Christianity

13. The Vision of a New Jerusalem 137
14. The Civics of Incarnation 147

Part VII

The Experience of Christianity

15. Christian Faith: The Experience of Prayer 153
16. Christian Hope: The Experience of the Future 163
17. Christian Love: The Experience of God 174

To Ken and Mose—
Christ-bearers to me—
Thanks

Introduction:
The Restless Animal

The flow of a man's life

Most of the time we live from day to day: not lives of quiet desperation perhaps, but at least lives that carry us onward in their drift like some huge river. And we float along with the current, seldom thinking about anything: where we are headed, why the river flows, what kind of flotsam or jetsam we might be. We pass much of our life this way and with good reason. For if we did not, we might never make any progress downstream.

Inevitably, however, it happens that bends or rapids crop up in the river. The current shifts, becomes unpredictable, and we are jarred, knocked about, sent shooting forward or caught in a whirlpool that threatens to drag us under. Shaken out of our complacency, we wonder. We cry out, we try to gain our feet, to stand up out of the river. And we ask questions whose answers may have seemed unimportant before. A nine-year-old girl dies of leukemia. A husband is slaughtered in an automobile accident. I fall in love with the most beautiful girl in the world. A young man wakes one morning to realize suddenly that he is a father, that one very weak baby has been given into his rough hands and is totally dependent upon him. At

1

such a moment the awesome question arises. What question? Any vital question, any question about life: Why are we here? Does life have any meaning? What is important in my life? Is death meaningful or is it merely senseless?

The vital question may occur during a great crisis, but often it arises for no reason at all. In either case it shakes us to our very depths. And it is no question easily answered: no simple answer of a few easy words will ease the yearning that has been stirred up. For we ask not in order to learn some bit of knowledge, but because the answer holds important consequences for our entire life: how we shall look at the world, the way we feel, what we consider good or bad, where we are going.

The persistence of life's question

The question is in each of us. It rises to the surface of our life in many different ways. Some men will spend their whole lives seeking an answer to satisfy the great question that drives them. Others only become aware of the question at a certain point of their life, at certain peak or crisis moments. And for them perhaps the question is easily answered. They find peace in the religion in which they were reared; they discover an answer in a life of social service or in the love of another person and the security of a family. Still other men suppress the question: should it ever arise in their lives they ignore it, brush it aside, or run until it is left far behind. But although the routine of daily living or the hedonism of drugs and alcohol may submerge the yearning, it still lurks in us, demanding an answer.

No ordinary question this. It is not just a question of the head or a matter of the stomach that can be satisfied through a simple word or a crust of bread. Our whole being is brought into question. If my child has been killed in a freak accident I want to know why; no pat intellectual answer about the inscrutable workings of the universe will satisfy my anger and rage against such a senseless tragedy.

Our yearning is not just a question of knowledge nor is it a longing of our senses. In the presence of beauty and joy we may, overwhelmed, momentarily forget the yearning within us but soon we will wonder again. What of this very beauty? Why is it here? Why does it speak to me so deeply? Yet what is its message that I only half hear?

Another person may quell this yearning and so I hope as I fall in love and lose my self and my question in the beloved. But soon again it rises to the surface. Human love is fragile. Often it breaks under the simple strains of daily living. Or in the middle of the night I awake to a vision of its fleetingness. For this love of mine, my shelter from life's cruelty and unconcern, is only human too. She shares the same fears, the same yearnings. Can we love and play in the sand only to die and have our frail castles washed away, our fleeting moments forgotten forever?

But perhaps I can build for the future. There are my children; they will be my hope and my faith. In them I shall not die; I shall not have lived in vain. And so I am triumphant until one day in

their eyes I perceive that dread yearning I have
known so well. And what shall I tell them, what
shall I give to them that will not disappoint or
disillusion?

This yearning and this restlessness, this insistent
question appears to be the only certainty we have
about ourselves. I am a man: I question. After that
silence? Perhaps we should take the question as
the center of our life. Is this man's greatness, that
he can never be satisfied, that he is ever driven on
to new heights, new peaks of experience? He is an
animal with a fatal disease, the dis-ease of his
eternal question, and this is his genius.

A noble stand! Heroic man against a cold world!
But if we live only for the question will we not in
the end despair? Such a purpose is insufficient. If
life be not more than a gritting of teeth to bear up
under the strain, it would well be ended sooner
than later. If there is no answer ultimately, then
our search now is meaningless. We are condemned
to frustration.

The religious search

We can neither ignore the question nor make the
question itself the final touchstone of our existence
unless we wish to court disaster and despair. The
question must set us off on a quest, and this quest
is a religious one. For religion is the element of
human existence where the question of meaning is
posed. Religion is the phenomenon that attempts to
interpret for us our question of meaning and then to
supply us with an experiential response to our question. The response is experiential because the ques-

tion itself demands such an answer: our yearning is not a matter only of the mind but of the heart and the nerves as well. The response of religion must minister to man as an entire complex human being.

But where shall we discover this religious answer? Few men indeed have come upon the answer for themselves. These few are the religiously gifted. They have had a direct insight into the problem. But the rest of us lack this intuition, and if we had to await one, we should probably never chance upon it. Fortunately the wait is unnecessary; answers to the yearning are easily available. For those religiously gifted men have communicated their insights, and from these men all men may have their quest fulfilled.

The end of our quest will lie in an experience of the world: an experience of fear or despair, of awe or love. And when we ask the religious man to share with us his answer, he will point toward his experience by means of a story. And in his story will lie an invitation to view the world with the eyes of the story. The story will speak to us on many levels; it will involve us as a total man, and if it seems to proffer a satisfaction of our longing we will enter into the world of the story and we will adopt that religious outlook.

The Christward vision

Our religious quest is for an ultimate reality which we can stand upon and which will give meaning and significance to our life. "Ultimate reality" is simply a more abstract and intellectual term for what men have everywhere spoken of as

God. Man's search for God has not changed so drastically during his time on earth. Perhaps he has become more intelligent and refined in his search, but the search itself is everywhere the same.

Christians believe that the principle of ultimate reality is a person rather than a thing or an abstract concept. And they believe that if man has searched for God in his religions, then, in Jesus of Nazareth, God has on his part come in search of man. In Jesus, God has provided man with the true and adequate answer to his quest. When the response of God in Jesus Christ encounters the quest of man for God, Christianity is born.

We now invite you to enter into the Christian experience, first through the stories and then through the rituals, ethics, institutions and dogmas which preserve this experience. Come look at life through a Christian's eyes, through the eyes of a man called Jesus. It is an exciting experience. Hopefully it will answer the feeling of yearning within you through its vision of life. It is an experience of fullness of life, overwhelming love and everlasting happiness. And it comes to perfection in a man Jesus who two thousand years ago left the trade of a carpenter in the little village of Nazareth in order to respond to the yearning within each of us.

Part I
The Stories of
Christianity

1

The Stories
of the Israelites

Christianity's story is of a man and a people, which is built in turn upon the story of a God and a nation. The man is Jesus and his people the Church; the God is Yahweh and his people the nation of Israel. Although we shall be principally concerned with Jesus, we can not ignore Israel, for the Christian experience arose out of Israel and her experience of God. So in answer to the vital question "What is the meaning of life?" a Christian would first relate the history of Israel.

The exodus from slavery

To this day every year at the great festival of Passover as each Jewish family gathers to eat the Passover supper, the youngest child in the family asks a question, "Why is this night different from all other nights?" In the answer lies the kernel of Israel's religion. The answer lies in an historical occurrence at the beginning of their history which has given the life of every Jew purpose and meaning.

Some three thousand years ago a leader rose up among a group of slaves in Egypt. This leader, whom tradition names Moses, led a revolt against the Pharaoh, Egypt's ruler. Heading the slaves, Moses inspired them to escape and flee Egypt. He called them to cast off their bondage of slavery. The slaves attributed their success in the escape to Moses' God. They experienced him as a God who had saved them from their taskmasters and had led them into freedom.

The exodus occurred during Israel's heroic age: about the same time as the Trojan war related in the Homeric epics. However when the story is first written down we are far from the age of Moses. The story of Moses, his God and the escape had been passed on carefully from generation to generation because in these events the people saw the birth story of their nation. During centuries of retelling naturally the narrative became more elaborate. Details were added. Dialogue between characters was invented. Certain episodes grew and took on tinges of the supernatural and miraculous.

The slaves had probably escaped, slipping out unnoticed at night. When Pharaoh discovered the ruse he set out in pursuit with his chariots. One of Egypt's boundaries was the Sea of Reeds, a marshy strip of land along the Sinai peninsula. Being on foot, the fugitives could walk through this marsh without becoming stuck, but Pharaoh's horses and chariots became embedded in the mud, and the slaves eluded their pursuers.

In the course of the ages these details were magnified in order better to impress upon the listener how great a victory God had brought about. The Sea of Reeds becomes the Red Sea, a different body of water altogether. Now Moses, standing at the edge of the Red Sea, prays to his God and stretches forth his hands. Miraculously the waters part, permitting the people to walk through the middle of the sea on dry land. When Pharaoh and his army attempt to follow, God causes the waters to rush together again, drowning the entire Egyptian army.

The importance of meaning

Such blatant elaboration shocks us. As modern men our primary concern is with what actually happened. Did these people go through the Red Sea or the Sea of Reeds? Did the waters part for them or not? If the first is the true account, then is not the embellished version not as valid, even false?

But we must remember that the ancient Israelites, retelling their story, were not concerned with the details so much as with the meaning of what had happened. They discovered that this historical event held a meaning for them which gave purpose to their life together. In the exodus they found a power, a God who rescued them and gave them freedom. Previously they had been slaves, now they were free. This freedom experience forms the story's central core; whatever strengthens its impact upon the reader is welcomed.

Looking at the story in terms of its central meaning, there is little difference between the version of what "actually" happened and the more elaborate, embellished account. The latter telling is even preferable since it communicates the message more forcefully and convincingly.

The God of the mountain

In the exodus event the people experienced their
God as a savior and a deliverer. But this was only
the beginning. The God of Moses now promises to
create out of this mass of slaves a new nation. Centuries later the Israelites remembered and relived
their nation's birth in the story of the giving of the
law to Moses on the top of Mount Sinai.

Escaping the Egyptian army, they had fled into
the wilderness and desert of the Arabian peninsula.
There, eventually, they pitched camp at the base of
the mountain and Moses went up into the mountain. There, amid thunders, lightnings and tremors
of the earth, as the later accounts describe it, God
made a covenant with the people.

This covenant or constitution set up a nation. A
set of laws was concluded between God, the ruler,
and his people by which a state was brought into
being and governed. The famous code of Ham-
murabi, formulated about the same time as Israel's
Law, is similar to Israel's covenant.

God reminds the people of what he has done for
them: he brought them out of Egypt and made
them free men. In return they owe him their obedience. Now, for their obedience God promises to
form them into a nation: a nation that shall endure
as long as the terms of the covenant are not broken.

A new experience of God emerges. The God
known to the people as their rescuer and deliverer
was now to become their ruler, their king. On
Mount Sinai is forged a constitution, a law for their

government. God will be their leader and ruler; he will lead them to a land they can occupy as their own. In return he demands to be worshiped as their sole God. Israel and its religion are grounded on this covenant, and throughout their history the Israelites will understand whatever happens to them in the light of this original covenant when God chose them to be his people.

Under Moses's successor, Joshua, the Israelites began to raid and plunder the land of Canaan, located approximately where modern Israel lies. A series of bloody wars ensue which continue for many generations until finally the native people are conquered and victory given to the Israelites. God has been faithful: he has given them the land.

Israel: a nation like all others

Once a landed nation, however, the Israelites soon forgot their original covenant with God. Adopting the local gods of Canaan, they are almost totally absorbed into the native population. Israel demands to have kings like the other nations, and her kings, like other monarchs, are concerned to consolidate their power and to build up wealth. Israel becomes a secular state: her old dependence upon the tribal Yahweh is soon forgotten.

The prophetic experience

During her period of prosperity another experience of God begins to develop. A series of prophets arise in Israel. These men, speaking in the name of God, call the people to return to the Lord and to his covenant. They accuse Israel of having violated the covenant upon which her existence is based.

But things are going well in Israel and the prophets' messages go unheeded. As time goes on, the message becomes more and more harsh. If the Israelites do not change their ways God will abandon them; he will no longer shield Israel but will deliver her up to her enemies.

The prophets experience God as all-powerful and as the controller of history. Slowly the idea develops that this God of Israel is more than simply one tribal God among many. He has control over all nations, not just Israel, but he loves Israel and her he has chosen. But now since Israel has abandoned God, he will in turn desert her.

And Israel soon collapses. Splitting first into two small nations, she is finally conquered by the Babylonians. Her land is burned and most of the people are deported into captivity in Babylonia. The dream of Israel had come to an end; gone is the glory and the power. Once again they are slaves, their freedom something to weep over. The God who once saved them has forsaken his people.

But even in exile the prophets continue to interpret to the people what is happening to them. In their prosperity and glory they had no use for God, so he has delivered them over to the enemy. Now in their captivity they may once more be ready to hear God and return to him.

The prophets saw Israel's defeat as a punishment for her failure to live up to the covenant. Now her captivity and slavery become means for purifying and remolding the people—during this time they once more realize their dependence upon God and they experience the power of God over all nations.

At the same time Israel begins to experience the mercy of God. In spite of everything he loves this people, and he is unable to forsake his nation forever. God does forgive, and after the captivity and the exile he will once again establish Israel as a nation. In her exile Israel learns hope. She learns that the future depends not on her but on God who has control of the future. And finally she begins to realize the great love of God. He can be wrathful and angry but he is also loving and ready to forgive.

Wisdom and hope

In addition to the prophets, Israel had other experiences of God. During her brief glory, Israel began to cherish the cultivation of wisdom. A group of men connected with the royal court devoted their lives to probing the implications of a good and God-fearing life. Proverbs and maxims were collected which guided the people in right living. And the wise men meditated upon the infinite wisdom of God that had brought into being the entire universe and that governs the life of men and nations.

The wisdom literature exhibits a deep knowledge. In it man confronts the questions that arise as he attempts to perceive God's influence upon the world. Why does God allow evil to flourish? Why are good men allowed to suffer? Through meditation upon such difficult problems Israel enriched her faith and came to experience more deeply the rich mystery of life. Her faith in God's guiding wisdom comes to fulfillment in Christianity, in Jesus whom Christians see as the incarnation of God's wisdom.

In Israel's suffering and exile another type of literature is born: apocalyptic. It speaks of crisis and disaster; it foretells the end of the nations in terrifying images of bloodshed, famine and desolation. But apocalyptic is really a literature of hope. For to the oppressed people it promised the collapse of their enemies' power. It offers the hope that God will again rescue his people and lead them out of slavery's darkness into the light.

Israel believed that her hope was fulfilled when the Persian king, Cyrus, restored Israel as a nation. But she never achieved a fraction of her former glory, and after a brief period of independence she is once again conquered, first by the Greeks, then by the Romans.

Her experience of apocalyptic hope in the future grows. Looking back on her past, she sees the image of her greatness in King David who brought her to the height of her power. Now in her weakness and helplessness, she hopes in the promises God made through his prophets: a new leader will come, as great if not greater than David. Under this new leader, whom the Jews refer to as the Messiah, once again God's people will witness greatness. Israel is subjected to Roman dominion but she eagerly awaits the Messiah, a new Moses to lead his people to freedom from slavery, a new David to bring back the glory of past days. During this period of waiting a man Jesus is born.

Israel's faith

Israel forms an insignificant power in world history. She only enjoys her brief period of glory under David because at that time there were no powerful neighbors around. She has produced little great art or thought compared to Greece or Rome. Her only fame is her experience of God. For Israel read her history, her glories and defeats, in terms of God. And in her history she comes to know this God intimately. He is first a savior, a God who brings man into freedom. Next at Sinai she comes to know and accept him as her king and ruler. As she proves faithless to the covenant, he shows himself as angry and as the controller not only of Israel's destiny but as the Lord of all peoples. When the nation is destroyed and carried off into exile, God becomes the comforter of his people. He becomes Lord of the future when he will once again bring his people from slavery to freedom. Finally, in his prophets, he shows himself as a force of love, fidelity and trust. Israel comes to know that she cannot depend upon herself or other men, but only upon God. Only he is worthy of obedience and loyalty. Only he will not finally disappoint.

Our quick retelling of Israel's story is merely a suggestion of the richness of her experience. Her full witness to that ex-

perience is found in the collection of books known to Christians as the Old Testament. There are her stories, her songs, her prophets' writings, the wisdom of her sages. We invite you to let these writings witness for themselves the experience they serve.

The stories of the exodus and of Sinai are presented most dramatically in Exodus 14:5-31 and Exodus 19 and 20.

Jeremiah's prophecies of doom and hope are found in Jeremiah 3:1-18.

Wisdom's song in Proverbs 8:22—9:18 shows the beauty of Israel's meditation on God.

And her future hope is seen in Isaiah 52:1-13.

2
The Stories
of Jesus

The state of Israel has been reduced to a province of the Roman Empire. The Jews maintain an uneasy relation with their conquerors: tension is always present and could flare out into the open at the slightest provocation. The Jewish people live on in the hope of a Messiah, a leader who will drive out the Romans and re-establish the glory of Israel. Many also believe the end of the world is near. They expect any day that events will occur which are sure signs of the end.

"A voice in the wilderness"

Into this situation comes a man named John. He refers to himself as "a voice crying in the wilderness," and he says his work is to "prepare the way of the Lord." He calls on the people to come back to God, to be sorry for their sins, to make amends and change their lives. The last days are here: God has already put the axe to the tree, and soon it will come crashing down.

John is a rough man: his is no message of comfort. He lives in the desert on a diet of locusts and honey; prophet seems to be the only appropriate description of him. Yet there have been no prophets for hundreds of years.

The man has a charisma and fascination about him and he picks up followers. They come and accept his ceremony of baptism. John stands in the middle of a stream and calls out to the people. Those who wish to change their lives, to be dedicated to God, come out to the prophet in the water. He submerges them in the stream as a sign that they wish to be cleansed of their sins and begin a new life.

One day as he is baptizing in the Jordan River a man presents himself to John for baptism. As John is about to perform the action, he suddenly stops, for there is something unusual about this man. Such a feeling of holiness pervades him that it almost seems possible to touch it. John hesitates. "Shouldn't you rather baptize me?" he asks. "Go on with the ceremony," replies the stranger. And John complies. After the rite the man walks out of the river and disappears again into the crowd.

The man and his message

The man is Jesus, a Jew, about thirty years old, from the small village of Nazareth. Soon after his baptism he begins to attract attention as a wandering teacher. He attracts to himself a small coterie of men and women who follow him around the countryside and look to him as their leader and teacher. Jesus and his band of disciples wander from village to village much as numerous other teachers were doing at the same time.

His message was similar to John the Baptist's. He spoke of an approaching kingdom of God, of a new day for Israel. He used much of the popular religious imagery of his day which considered the world near its end. He demanded a change of heart from the people: a change of heart based on the principle of love: love for God and love for one's brother. He spoke of God as a Father, and he wanted all men to come to the realization that they were all children of God and therefore brothers of one another.

In addition Jesus had the power of healing. He was able to restore sight to men who had been blind since birth. A Roman centurion came to him once to ask for his help. His son was sick and could die. Would Jesus please help the boy? Jesus simply tells the centurion that his son will recover, and miraculously the boy, far away at home, recovers at that instant.

A sign of contradiction

Given his message and his healing powers, Jesus should have been extremely popular. After all there is nothing more true, even trite, than to speak of the brotherhood of man and the fatherhood of God. One modern theologian has gone so far as to call the phrase by its initials, BOMFOG. The message is innocuous. Further, a man reported to possess curative powers should never lack for an audience.

But this wandering preacher has certain personality traits and a slant on things that does not sit well with many. John the Baptist has been thrown into prison and beheaded in reward for his work, and Jesus was not so naive as to suspect that he would be received differently.

To speak of the brotherhood of man is fine as long as one remains at the level of generalities. But Jesus quickly moves into specifics, and he often concludes by denouncing the way of life of the Pharisees and the Scribes, two powerful classes in Jewish society. He sides openly with the poor, the beggars, the sick, and other undesirable elements of his society. He does not preach a revolution by violent overthrow of the state, but in a time of tense Jewish nationalism he could easily be interpreted as seditious toward Rome.

In addition to his proclivity for the lower strata of society he has a righteousness and cocksureness about him guaranteed either to make one believe in him and what he says or to make one detest him. No one remains non-committal. He is a forceful and dynamic figure, not afraid to assert something simply on the basis of his own authority. He has no doubts that he is completely right, and he employs little tact in confronting those he feels are wrong and in need of reform. It is little wonder that the Jewish leaders of the day found him an extremely dangerous fellow and soon began to plot his death when they saw his potential popularity and success.

Trial and death

Inevitably he is arrested and tried by both the Jewish leaders on religious grounds and by the Roman leaders on political grounds. He is convicted and sentenced to death. According to Roman custom he is first scourged with whips and then crucified. He is nailed to a cross between two thieves and left there until dead.

The crowd of people as usual plays fickle. Five days before his arrest they had granted him a hero's welcome into Jerusalem; at the trial itself they clamor for his death. His coterie of men and women followers for the most part desert him. The men flee the scene and only the women are brave enough to stand by him till the end.

We can easily imagine the feelings of these disciples. They had each met Jesus and immediately felt their life changed by him. Eagerly they had abandoned their occupations, their homes, even their families, and to travel with him they were content to live like vagabonds. The future was glorious because this man obviously could transform the world. But as they came to know him better they grew less sure just who he was or what he would accomplish. Some expected he would be more political; perhaps he would organize a band of men to overthrow the government as previous leaders had tried. Others hoped his preaching of love, brotherhood, and a return to God might touch all men's lives as it had touched their own. The one thing they could not foresee was total humiliation and defeat: Jesus himself might have imagined this but his disciples were not so insightful.

Just as success seems assured and the entire populace of Jerusalem is about to rally about Jesus, he is suddenly arrested and condemned with no one to plead his case. Indeed, he himself seems to acquiesce in the decision.

Three years dissipate within one week. Small

wonder these men lost their reason and fled the whole scene like frightened children. Not many have made such great sacrifices for a noble cause or altered their entire life style for the sake of such a commitment. When this ideal is suddenly shattered before one's eyes, the whole world blurs, nothing makes sense, reality takes on the quality of nightmare.

One numb day, the Jewish Sabbath, or day of rest, passes. The men are either still in hiding within the city of Jerusalem or they have already fled the city and gone back to Galilee to pick up the pieces.

The dawn of new life

The women, on the morning after the Sabbath, go to visit the grave. Words only go so far to communicate what they experienced there. First the women and after them Peter, the head apostle, and finally the other disciples discover that this man who died two days ago is not dead but alive. How do they know? Because they meet him and as a result of that encounter they *know* that he is not dead but alive.

"He has risen from the dead!" they cry. But this way of speaking only begins to point to the profound reality they experienced. When modern men think of someone rising from the dead, they think of a corpse opening his eyes, rising and walking about. Such a concept does not adequately describe the resurrection.

Jesus is not merely resuscitated: he is resurrected

and death lies vanquished at his feet. Resurrection
for the Jews meant something that would not hap-
pen until the end of the world. Then God would
raise men from the dead and the glorious reign of
God upon earth would begin. Jesus' resurrection
told his disciples that that reign of God had begun.

The resurrection stories preserved by the Church
are not journalistically accurate accounts of what
happened. They are more concerned to communicate the good news of death's conquest than a
scientific description of Jesus' resurrected body. But
Christians through the centuries have agreed that
these stories capture the experience of that Sunday
as well as any human words can. The band of men
and women who had had their lives shattered on
Friday now were convinced that Jesus' death signaled not the end but the beginning. He had died,
and in dying he had conquered death. Now he was
alive never to die again.

The meaning of resurrection

The disciples believed that Jesus himself, not
merely his ideals or his spirit, lives on. They speak
of their experience in terms of seeing him, even
touching him. Jesus' appearances are miraculous
but they are described in material images: seeing,
touching, hearing, eating.

But resurrection is not an end in itself: it is an
event which brings meaning into man's life. And
it produced an extraordinary change in the life of
each disciple. On Friday they had run away in

fear and cowardice, their dream of the past three years shattered. On Easter to a man they place their lives in the service of Jesus and his message. This service will cost most of them their lives. They die cruelly and far from their homes, but they die in joy even with the realization that at least one of their hopes (the end of the world and the return of Jesus) has not been fulfilled. The only explanation for this new courage is the meaning they derived from Jesus' conquest of death.

In the end all we have is the testimony and consequent lives of these men and women. We cannot prove the resurrection one way or another. It calls each man and woman to accept or reject it. It forms the center of the Christian faith, and Christians throughout two thousand years have chosen to live out their lives in its light. For Christians believe that Jesus' rising from the dead provides man with an interpretation of the world, of themselves, of each other and of God.

The stories not only invite belief, but they also seem to possess a power to create belief in them; they convince and draw men into their framework. Christians offer these stories of Jesus to the world as an invitation to enter into them and to share the experience of eternal life found in them.

The core of Jesus's teaching can be found in the "Sermon on the Plain" of Luke's Gospel (Luke 6).

Jesus' controversy with the Pharisees is seen in Luke 20.

The earliest telling of his arrest and crucifixion is found in Mark 14—15.

In Matthew 28 is the story of the women at the tomb on Sunday morning.

A story of the disciples' commissioning is found in Luke 24:36-53.

3

From Experience
to Expression

The Gospel writers

When the disciples had encountered their risen
Lord, they immediately wanted to tell everyone the
great news. When we have had a tremendous
experience, when something fantastic has happened
to us, when our life has been wondrously transformed, we want desperately to communicate this
experience to others. And we relay the experience
best through telling our story, what happened to us.

The disciples were no different. They communicated to people their experience of Jesus by relating
what Jesus had done. But now as they looked back
on Jesus' life and ministry, certain events are seen
in a different light. Now looking back, Jesus' life
shimmers in the transforming experience of his
resurrection. The disciples now realize that this man
Jesus is truly God himself, and in his earthly life
they now perceive glimpses of his divinity to which
they had been blind before.

Although the four Gospels narrate incidents of
Jesus' life, they are not biographies in the modern
sense, just as the stories of the exodus are not

modern history. The disciples are more interested in the meaning of Jesus' life and its impact for human existence than in the bare facts. They are more concerned with the Jesus whom they experience now, living and working in them and in other Christians, than in isolating what happened thirty years ago as he walked the shores of Galilee.

The Gospels are not the biography of a dead man, but of a man still alive in the fullest sense of the word. He is alive in his followers, he acts through them, and through them he continues his ministry, his teaching and his healing. The Gospels are witnesses to the experience of the living Jesus; they view his earthly ministry from the vantage point of the current living experience of Jesus in the Christian community.

When we read the Gospels we are reading of the experience Jesus has on the writer's life *as he writes:* in Jesus' life, teaching, example, death and resurrection the evangelist has discovered the answer to his vital question. He has experienced in this man a God who loves men so much that he was willing to become a man and die for their sake. He has found that the way to approach his fellow man is as a brother and in love. He knows that he can call the maker of the universe his Father, and that the world did not simply chance to occur nor is it the product of some force, impersonal or even inimicable to us. He knows that now there is a purpose to human life: we are not flickering flames soon to be extinguished forever. Our enemy, death, the thing we most fear and the reality most inevitable and unavoidable, will not be the end of us. We shall pass beyond death and we shall live.

To keep this treasure

The early Christians were all Jews, and the experience they received from Jesus built upon the experience of God and reality they had already come to know in Israel's stories. Jesus became the ultimate and decisive experience of reality, but he built upon and brought to perfection the older traditions. There is a sharpening of focus and a refinement of the Israelite experience in Jesus as well as the decisive event of his resurrection.

So when the Christians set about collecting the various writings which definitively captured their experience of life, they adopted the stories of the Jewish religion and then selected those stories and writings about Jesus and the Christian experience which most perfectly caught and communicated that experience.

As the years passed, the danger of losing the purity of Jesus' vision arose and a list of writings was drawn up by the communities to serve as a norm of the experience. This guaranteed that as the centuries rolled on these selected writings could be used to reach the true experience of Jesus, and they could also be employed to evaluate the contemporary community's faith in terms of the primitive expression. In other words, the Christian community of the year 1200 could come to the original experience of the disciples through these writings, and at the same time they could judge how authentically their own experience of Jesus compared with the original faith.

The holy book

These writings became known as Scripture or the Bible. Christian Bibles are divided into two sections: the Old Testament contains the writings and stories of Israel, and the New Testament the writings and stories of Jesus. Each Testament consists of a number of separate books written at different times. For example, in the Old Testament there are books detailing the history of Israel, books of poetry, books written by Israel's wise men, and books collecting the sayings and lives of the prophets. The New Testament begins with the four Gospels, then the Acts of the Apostles (a history of the first days of the Church which captures the early Christian experience), various letters written by different disciples and Church leaders to Christian communities, and, finally, a book of apocalyptic that provided hope for the early Christians during their time of persecution.

A living tradition

Catholic Christians believe that the Bible is the authentic source and controller of our experience, yet Christian faith is living and not confined to a book. Jesus appeared to his disciples and his resurrection message was passed to other men in different times and places through these disciples and the men who succeeded them. Jesus lives in the community that calls itself by his name and participates in his life and experience. The Bible came into existence out of this living community, and it properly belongs to this community. It cannot be divorced from the center of lived Christian experience. The Bible contains Jesus' experience in its most authentic expression and communication: it is truly the Word of God for Christians. But it has its life only for the community gathered together in Jesus' name: for there among men is God truly found.

Part II
The Dogmas of
Christianity

4

To the Depths
of Meaning

The spread of the good news

After the resurrection, the disciples spread the good news that they discovered in this man and his life: the good news of a God who cares for us and who saves us from death, the good news of a goal for living found in loving—God's love for us and our love for God and our fellow man. But as they attempted to communicate their experience they found they had to struggle with words and their meaning.

They began by telling about their Lord. They told how he died and how God did not forsake him but raised him from the dead. But almost immediately they needed to articulate their experience more fully. A religious experience affects and transforms man's whole life, his entire way of looking at things. It cannot be relegated to some little corner and brought out into the open only when useful or needed.

These disciples are no longer the same as they were before. A new experience has entered their lives, and they must now reorder their existence in the light of Jesus. Consider what happens when a couple marries. Both persons must reorient their lives and habits. Before, each had only himself to consider, but now they are no longer one: they are two.

First the disciples had to understand what the resurrection meant about Jesus. What impact does this event have on the lives and the deaths of the rest of mankind? Who is this Jesus that God should resurrect him? Does his death have a meaning in the light of his resurrection? Such probes into the meaning of their new experience give birth to Christian theology. A Greek word meaning "talk of God," theology is the attempt to explain in precise language the meaning found in the Christian experience.

A search for precision

The first centuries of the Christian religion are overflowing with different theologies, different ways of understanding the experience of Jesus. Again the most obvious parallel is the experience of love between a man and a woman. They experience their love for one another, but they also wish to talk about it, to describe it. One may be a poet and succeed in capturing the love in a poem. An outsider reading the poem will experience an inkling of their love. But the poem is not intellectually but rather experientially precise: it does not explain; it, too, merely *is*. A poem can capture but it does not explain the experience. It is as mysterious as the original love. So the lover may try to put his experience into more precise words: he talks of his love in terms of philosophy or biology or psychology. And employing the precise terms of these disciplines, he might arrive at a precise definition of his love.

But although he gains in precision when he uses scientific words, he at the same time loses the vividness of the original experience. Love can be examined in terms of philosophy or psychology, but each only captures for examination a fragment of the original experience. A poem might actually awaken in the reader a glimpse of love; a scientific analysis explains the experience in part but it cannot kindle it in another.

The Christian, too, wishes to delve into his experience, to mine its riches and bring it to intellectual awareness so that he may discuss it, deal with it, and enable it to penetrate to all points of his existence. Because he is a man, gifted with intellect, he desires to articulate his experience. He wishes to bring it to mind so that he may evaluate it beside other experiences. He cannot avoid theology any more than he could avoid the vital question in the beginning.

An experience as infinitely rich and important to satisfy man's yearning sparks many different explanations. Men try to get hold of the core experience in words, and just as they think they have hold of it, they realize their expression is still inadequate. So they try again, either refining the original formulation, or, if that proves a dead end, taking a new approach to the problem.

The disciples had to articulate their experience at least adequately enough to enable other men to come to the experience. And they had to be able

to talk to both their Jewish contemporaries and to
the Greek world at large about this experience. How
does it differ from other men's experience of life?
How is it better than other ways of looking at the
world? What in the present world-view of a Greek
or a Jew will help him understand the Christian
experience? These are extremely difficult questions,
and it is no surprise that the early years of the
Christian faith are filled with attempted answers
and vigorous refutations of what were considered
wrong answers.

The birth of Christian theology

The New Testament evidences Christianity's earliest theologies throughout its pages. The Gospels
represent profound attempts to articulate the experience of Jesus through a telling of his life. But
the main source for nascent theology lies in the
letters to the New Testament churches, and particularly the letters of the apostle Paul. Paul is,
after Jesus himself, the most influential person in
Christianity. Christian experience originates in Jesus
and was given shape by the first Christian communities whose testimony forms our New Testament.
Pre-eminent of the New Testament witnesses is
Paul—the most influential and perhaps the greatest
Christian theologian. He is represented in the New
Testament far more than any other author, and his
thought brought Christianity into the Greek world.

Paul enters a Christianity that still considers itself
part of Judaism, and he makes it a religion in its
own right and translates its experience into language understandable outside of its original Jewish

context. The civilized world of his day was that of Greece and Rome. Judaism was a small religion on the fringes of that world. Paul helped Christianity succeed by translating his experience of Jesus into terms understandable to a citizen of the Roman Empire. Here was his genius, and under his impetus Christianity within three hundred years had become *the* religion of the Roman Empire.

Paul began a task of theology which has continued to the present day: translating the unique Christian experience into terms intelligible to contemporary man. Theology forms a bridge between a culture or civilization and Christian faith. It is always an attempt, and being an attempt it can and does fail. Naturally, today we can learn from 2,000 years of theological practice. Christianity has been hammered out on the anvils of countless cultures and philosophies. But in its early days theology was a dangerous enterprise. The young Church clung to an experience which she was extremely anxious and zealous not to lose. But every attempt at articulation posed the danger of warping, distorting, or even betraying the original experience.

The Church soon gathered up those documents which truly and perfectly transmitted and captured her experience. These she made her safeguard, her measure by which to judge any subsequent statement. This collection forms the Bible. But inadequate understandings soon arose and in order to preserve her experience from distortion she was forced to formulate expressions opposed to those which betrayed the experience.

Ultimate expressions of this kind are called dogmas. Dogma is usually defined by the Church when the truth of the experience is in danger of being wrongly understood. It forms a corrective. It does not add to the faith: rather it secures and preserves it.

The Church has the power and right to propound dogmas only because she is the recipient of that original Easter experience. The disciples, receiving the experience, conveyed it to other men. Communities grew up which lived and thought their lives from within that experience. Through these communities, these churches, the unique Christian experience is passed on. Only they know and live it; only they can judge concerning it.

When the great crises arose in the early Church, the question was often solved through a council: a gathering of all Church leaders, the successors of Jesus' disciples. The council examined the problem and in prayer attempted to formulate a solution true to the faith which had been handed down to them. The conciliar decisions then became the decision of the entire Christian people. Often these dogmas were published in the form of a creed, and this creed served as a guide for interpreting the faith and the stories of Jesus.

  The Church Praying

The Creed of Nicea:

We believe in one God,
the Father, the Almighty,
maker of heaven and earth,
of all that is seen and unseen.

We believe in one Lord, Jesus Christ,
  the only Son of God,
  eternally begotten of the Father,
  God from God, Light from Light,
  true God from true God,
  begotten, not made, one in Being with the Father.
  Through him all things were made.
For us men and for our salvation
  he came down from heaven:
by the power of the Holy Spirit
  he was born of the Virgin Mary, and became
  man.
For our sake he was crucified under Pontius Pilate;
  he suffered, died, and was buried.
  On the third day he rose again
  in fulfillment of the Scriptures;
  he ascended into heaven
    and is seated at the right hand of the Father.
He will come again in glory to judge the living
    and the dead,
  and his kingdom will have no end.
We believe in the Holy Spirit, the Lord, the giver
    of life,
  who proceeds from the Father and the Son.
With the Father and the Son he is worshiped and
    glorified.
He has spoken through the prophets.
We believe in one holy, catholic and apostolic
    Church.
We acknowledge one baptism for the forgiveness of
    sins.
We look for the resurrection of the dead
    and the life of the world to come. Amen.

5

The Foundations of Christology

Of the many dogmas that have been formulated in the course of Christianity's long history, two are central to the Christian experience. These two dogmas define the very heart of Christian belief in Jesus and they are central to all the forms of the Christian faith. They answer the problem of Jesus' identity and his task: who was he and what did he accomplish?

The God who became man—incarnation

Every New Testament author wrestled with the question of Jesus' identity, and the issue was not finally and definitively solved until the Council of Chalcedon four centuries later. But the point at issue was more one of refinement and precision than a broad issue of Jesus' nature. The Christian community from Easter Sunday on has been convinced and has lived in the belief that Jesus was truly God without ceasing to be truly man.

The history of Israel was an education of a nation by God. Throughout their history, God prepares this people. He chooses them, delivers them from slavey, makes them a nation, gives them over to their enemies when they forsake him, and sends them prophets to call them back to him.

Finally, in the day of Jesus, God himself appears on earth—not as God but as a man like any man. The disciples who had lived with him lacked no conviction of Jesus' humanity. He grew tired. He became irritable. He could wax enthusiastic and grow discouraged also. Perhaps they sensed a special unique quality about him, but they never doubted that he was a man like them, and when he hung on the cross they never hoped to see him alive again.

In Jesus' resurrection the disciples began to realize that merely to call Jesus a man did not accurately describe him. This man was in some significant way different from the rest of men. A mere man could not possibly conquer death. Not even Moses or the greatest prophets had escaped death. Only God would be able to conquer death. And as they prayed to God for guidance and wisdom and as they reflected upon Jesus and his words, they were led under God's guiding influence to see that God had been working in Jesus in an entirely unique and astounding way. This man Jesus *was* God himself.

Certain incidents now made greater sense. This man spoke with authority; he dared do things no good Jew would presume to do, things seemingly against God's law. But if Jesus were God enfleshed in man, then his words *had* authority and were not blasphemous or presumptuous. His words would lead away from certain dead ends of the Jewish religion and back to a vital experience of God. The disciples knew that the words had divine authority when Jesus' teaching was confirmed and sealed by his resurrection.

One of the earliest Christian doctrines relates directly to the incarnation. The early Christians held that Jesus' birth was miraculous: his mother had conceived although she was a virgin. By this dogma Christians confessed that Jesus had been both divine and human from the beginning. He was not adopted by God as his Son at some point during his life or at his resurrection. On the other hand, he was completely human inasmuch as he was born from a woman; not a God descended from the sky, he partakes fully in our humanity. The dogma of the virgin birth preserves Jesus' unity as well as his twofold nature by grounding the incarnation in a concrete happening.

The doctrine of the incarnation (God-made-man) lies at the center of Christianity. Jesus becomes the focus because in himself he is both man and God. He forms a bridge between man and God, reconciling the two within himself and uniting God and man forever. His unique unrepeatable life forever eliminates the possibility that either God or man can completely be divorced or forget about or abandon one another. As God became man to show himself to us as love and forgiveness, so Jesus as a man accepted the invitation.

This doctrine cannot be totally explained: it remains on the plane of mystery. At the core, it says that the chasm between God and man exists no longer. Why should God have become man? No compelling reason—only out of love. But that it happened has been the witness of Christians everywhere from the world's first Easter.

When early Christians attempted to probe the

mystery more deeply, to explain it more, they fell into many errors. The mystery holds together two statements. Jesus is truly a man, and Jesus is truly God. Jesus' divinity should not be overemphasized lest the man become a puppet or a mask. Emphasize his humanity too much and his uniqueness as God is lost. Nor should his personality be split: God one minute and man the next. He does not lie in his crib as an infant and from that crib contemplate how he made the world. Somehow in God's wisdom and power Jesus does not cease to be a man in every sene of our humanity even though he is truly God.

The death that won life—atonement

If Jesus is God-become-man, then his life, what he said, and what he did assume enormous importance. And the early Christians found in Jesus the culmination and the perfection of the Jewish experience of God. For thousands of years this people had been growing slowly to know God. The Old Testament is filled with glimpses of this God and of what he wants to say to men. It was his education and building of relations with men.

In Jesus the decisive breakthrough occurs. In this man are summed up all the teachings of Jewish history about the God who saves, all the prophets' words about a God who wants to draw near to man and to lead man toward him, all the longings of Israel's poets to sing and pray to, and celebrate worthily, this God, and all the writings of her wise men who showed Israel how to live in accord with God's infinite wisdom. Christians recognized Jesus as God's wisdom, his glory, his Word, even God himself. And his teachings about the love of God and man summed up and gave confirmation to the entire Jewish faith.

But Jesus went beyond the Jewish experience as well. And Christians saw in his death a unique and unparalleled act. It was unbelievable to the Jews that God would become a man and walk the earth with them, but that he would also die for them was absolutely unthinkable. This God shatters all conventions and expectations: he refuses to act as a God should.

In Jesus' seemingly senseless death, Christians soon saw a meaning. In the light of his resurrection and victory over death they perceived a more perfect repetition of the escape from Egypt. There God had delivered the slaves from their captivity. But in Jesus' death and resurrection God delivers all mankind from the slavery of sin and death. A guilty mankind nailed an innocent man to the cross. This man had come preaching love, and we could not stand his message. To stop him we killed him, pounding nails through soft flesh. We refused his love and preferred to live in silence, hating or at best tolerating one another. But the power of love was so strong that it broke through both the violence of our guilt and sin and the chains of death and the grave. Love won and freed us from the curse of our pride and isolation in spite of our obstinacy.

In the incarnation God broke through the barrier between himself and man by becoming a man. In Jesus' death and resurrection he led us into freedom, not from human masters, but from the greatest enemies: sin, which makes it impossible for us to live in peace with one another, and death, which continually tells us everything we do is in vain.

God broke through both barriers, and on the cross his love proved that his commitment to us can never fail, die or be broken. We are now at one with God through his death on the cross whether we are aware of the glorious news or not. The battle is won—love *has* conquered division and death. All that remains now is that all men everywhere become aware of this at-one-ment and come to experience the Christian joy.

The answer to our life's vital question is not a program of what we should do—it is the good news of what has already been done. Jesus slew death and broke the wall separating us from our true happiness. God's only adequate name is Love, and Jesus has brought love to us and made it possible to love one another because he has freed us forever from the enemies of love: sin, guilt, envy, anger, death.

It is impossible to understand the inner dynamics of the atonement completely. But whenever Christians have allowed the Easter experience to mold their lives, whenever they have taken to their hearts the resurrection stories, whenever they have entered into the Easter rituals, then they have found it possible to overcome the destructiveness of sin in their lives and live at peace with their fellow man; for them death has no longer held a fear. Man is free right now; why then does he live as through he were still in chains?

Incarnation:

Luke's account of the virgin birth is found in the first two chapters of his Gospel.

Paul in his letter to the Philippians quotes an ancient Christian hymn on the incarnation (Philippians 2:6-11).

The hymn at the beginning of John's Gospel is the most sublime expression of the incarnation (John 1:1-18).

Atonement:

Acts 13:17-39 reports a speech by Paul on what Jesus accomplished.

Paul's theology of the atonement reaches its apex in Romans 5:12-21.

Colossians 1:21-23 contains a later Christian development of atonement theology.

Part III
The Rituals of
Christianity

6

The Drama of Worship

Walk into Easter

Stories at best are only an invitation to enter into the Christian outlook; they make faith appealing but they cannot communicate it in all its richness. Stories appeal to us primarily as listeners. At best a story can compel us to enter into it, but only imaginatively: our body remains relatively uninvolved. While our mind enters the lands and vistas of the tale, our body remains seated in front of the storyteller, or holding a book in front of us, or watching a screen.

But the Christian experience works upon and transforms the whole man. We have to enter body and soul into the Easter morning event: just as the apostles, we must be eye-witnesses to this event. Such witnessing is possible through ritual. Ritual is drama where we are actors rather than audience. In ritual we act out certain key dramas related to Jesus in order to bring Jesus, his outlook, his experience into our own lives. As Paul said, we "put on Jesus," we shape our lives, the story we tell, in accordance with Jesus' story.

Ritual involves worship. For most of us worship

means going to church, saying our prayers or getting down on our knees. But these are only the externals of worship. We come closer to the true nature of worship if we think of it as admiration and imitation. When we find a person we admire, we want to incorporate something of that person into our own lives. Children imitate more consciously than adults. A small boy will often attempt to be just like his father. He will walk like him or talk like him; when he sits down in a chair he will cross his legs just like dad. He admires his father and he then copies and imitates him to capture in his own life what he admires.

This phenomenon persists in a more unconscious form throughout adulthood. We only grow and change by imitating a role until it becomes natural. If we admire Jesus and the way he saw the world, we want to incorporate into our own lives the manner in which he approached life. And we can do that through imitation and admiration. When we admire and attempt to copy him we are worshiping him.

In ritual and worship we act out certain actions which help us to appropriate into our lives traits and qualities we find admirable in Jesus' life. Christians feel that only by assimilating themselves to Jesus can they be happy and fulfilled. If Jesus is truly God living as man, then his vision of life is the perfect vision; his way of dealing with his fellow men and with God is the true way; his way of living leads to the fullest life, the life that death does not end.

Christian worship includes praise and adoration, thanksgiving and petition. All these activities bring the worshiper into closer relationship to God. We adore God because of his greatness, because of his love for us, because of his goodness—because in the last analysis he is God. We give him thanks for what he has done for us. We thank him for the beauty of the story he has unfolded in Israel and in Jesus. We thank him for the breathless awe we feel when we stand before his creation: the brightness of a sunrise, the majesty of a mountain, the silence of a remote pond, the dignity of a river. And we petition him for our own needs, the needs of all those dear to us, and for all men.

Christian worship is our school. It is the way we become acquainted with the stories and the person of God. Worship involves our response to God through adoration, thanksgiving and petition. But it also contains God's response to us: a reminder of what he has done in the past, and, in his sacraments, a making real and present his love and care for us today.

In worship we learn about God. If we had only the stories and dogmas we might think them true, but they would not touch us deeply, they would not change our lives significantly. God and his love for us would remain mostly an intellectual knowledge. We might realize that he loves us but we could not feel or experience that love. Nor would we be able to grow, deepen and mature in that love. For if love is to grow it must be experienced in all its vitality between the two lovers.

We might confess that God was a living, dynamic God but there would be no way for us to feel him alive in our own lives. In worship we do encounter the living God. We come to know him as we learn what he has done and as we experience what he is doing in our lives now. And finally, because we come to know him, we grow to love him and want to imitate him. And in the holy play of worship as we re-enact what he has done we bring into our own lives the experience of Jesus. And when we experience the world this way, when we see it through his eyes, have we not become like Jesus?

 The Church Praying

Hymn of Praise

Glory to God in the highest,
*   and peace to his people on earth.*
Lord God, heavenly King,
almighty God and Father,
*   we worship you, we give you thanks,*
*   we praise you for your glory.*
Lord Jesus Christ, only Son of the Father,
Lord God, Lamb of God,
you take away the sin of the world
*   have mercy on us;*
you are seated at the right hand of the Father:
*   receive our prayer.*
For you alone are the Holy One,
you alone are the Lord,
you alone are the Most High,
*   Jesus Christ,*
*   with the Holy Spirit*
*   in the glory of God the Father. Amen.*

Symbols: clusters of meaning

Jesus' life and teachings hold the key to living in and understanding the world. In this man lies the meaning of life, and this meaning is contained in certain symbols.

A symbol is a focus of meaning. It contains within itself a meaning. We cannot live without symbols and man could be defined as a symbolic animal. For he is an animal that seeks for meaning, lives for meaning and cannot exist without meaning. Anything that has meaning for man or says something to him is a symbol. Symbols include clocks, pictures, water, fire, a handshake, a kiss, and of course words themselves. Because symbols contain meaning within them they become centers of power.

Made meaningful in nature

Some things are symbols merely because men have agreed that they shall signify something. A stop sign brings us to a halt simply because our society has decided it should. Such symbols are more properly called signs and will not occupy our attention.

But other symbols carry an intrinsic meaning, not merely a meaning we have imposed upon it. A stop sign in itself carries only an arbitrary meaning. But water, fire, and the concept of "word" carry a meaning in themselves. True they have a meaning for man only because man seeks meaning. But we have not given these symbols their meaning. Rather the meaning we find there resides in them already. Water means both life and death because we need it to live and we die from its lack or by drowning. But we have not imposed this meaning upon water; the meaning resides in the water simply by the nature of things.

Such symbols have a power in them: they bring to us a meaning beyond ourselves. Through these symbols we can enter into a relationship with our world: the world itself takes on meaning for us. Meaning is not limited to our minds and intellects but it can be found in the world about us. It is not just the case that we need to have meaning in order to live and so we impose it on our lives and our world. No, these great symbols of water or fire speak to us of a meaning that does not depend solely upon ourselves.

Christian rituals make use of our natural symbols such as fire, word and water. Christianity takes the natural symbols and builds upon them. It is an enrichment of our life: through our experience of Jesus we are made more human, we become more as God wishes man to be; we become more ourselves. All of us have some meaning in our lives, some meaning that derives from natural symbols. Who cannot feel reborn with the return of spring? The cold snows melt away and we await eagerly the first flush of green, the first color returned to a dead world. And gradually the world comes alive again until it bursts in an orgy of flowers and rainbow colors. Spring is a natural symbol, and men have always read that symbol as rebirth.

Made history in Israel

The natural symbols found both in nature and in man himself (such as love and forgiveness) were taken up into Israel's experience of God. But in Israel the symbols take on a new quality as they are drawn into Israel's history. For Israel experienced God primarily in the events of her life and her history. In history she perceived the power of God working. The natural symbols were drawn into the historical drama. And because they became part of Israel's sacred history their natural power or potential for meaning increased.

Made flesh in Jesus

Jesus builds upon the religious experience of Israel. He took up into himself the diverse strands of Israel's insights and once again transformed them, enriching their meaning, making them more universal, bringing their power for man to perfection. In Jesus these great symbols, natural to man and made historical in Israel's experience, reach to the very heart of reality. Their meaning is purified and enriched to such a degree that they become powerful enough to transform man's life. The different symbols group together in new relationships around the person of Jesus. They form and enrich themselves according to his experience. And they are then passed into the Christian community, where they are embedded in dramatic actions relating to Jesus. These symbolic dramas are so powerful in meaning, so able to transform the man who comes in contact with them, that they receive a new name: sacraments.

The encounter of sacrament

Through the sacraments man enters into the Christian experience. Through their drama and symbols it is possible for a man to meet Jesus Christ at certain important crucial moments of his life. These crucial moments are familiar to all of us; they are moments when the vital question often arises: moments when the everyday world recedes from our vision and suddenly we are face to face with the great mystery of life: moments of birth, of growth, of sickness and healing, moments of vocation and choosing a course in life. These are gifted moments when life can take on a strange mystery and beauty, when we are open to the possibility of a deep meaning in our life. At such times we are open to encounter Jesus and his vision.

These powerful sacramental actions have the ability to plunge us into Jesus and transform us into his likeness. They exist to mediate Jesus to us; they bring us into contact with him so that, just as in his own lifetime in Palestine, he is able today to infuse us with his message, heal our wounds both physical and spiritual, nourish us in the life we share with him, and build us into his body. One of Paul's primary images of the Church was the body of Christ. Jesus lives on in the Church which is the continuation of his life, his message, his ministry and his vision here on earth. The sacramental actions occur within his Church, and they are truly acts of the Church in the name of her Lord. The sacraments exist for the benefit of Christians, so that those living today can meet and be healed by Jesus just as the people of his day could.

But if the sacraments exist in the Church and for the Church, their power is meant for the entire world. Israel experienced God as the God of one nation; Jesus teaches men a God of all mankind. Jesus' mission of teaching and healing was for all men. Similarly every Christian enters into that mission.

The sacraments plunge men into Jesus' experience so that they may grow into him, be healed by him, and witness for him. But the sacrament does not end with the encounter. It transforms and heals so that Christians might be able to carry the good news of deliverance and healing to the rest of men.

Although it is the source of his life, ritual for a Christian is never the end. Always he is sent forth from the sacrament commissioned to bring evidence and signs of his experience into the world. As the sacrament transforms the individual Christian into another Christ, so the Christian in turn receives the power and the commission to make Christ's presence felt in the world. Jesus did not exist for himself but for his fellows. If they would be true, Christians cannot help but live for their neighbor.

7

Sacraments of Initiation —Baptism and Confirmation

The sacraments of baptism and confirmation stand at the door to Christian experience. They introduce men to that experience by plunging men into the death and resurrection and then commissioning them to carry the Easter faith into the world.

Natural meanings

First we must examine the three natural symbols associated with baptism and confirmation: water, fire and oil. Each has a powerful natural meaning in itself which is infinitely enriched by association with Jesus and his experience.

Stand before the sea and think—of time and eternity, of power in storms and soothing life-bringing breezes. Look back into the past; before men or animals, before even fish or plants, there was the sea. Older than any living thing it is the source of our life. "The river is within us; the sea is all about us." What is our blood, our symbol for life, but a river flowing within us? We came from the eternal sea, and often we dream of returning to that same sea, of going down to the sea in ships or alone to be washed clean and rocked in motherly arms where we can forget the land and the life behind.

Water has always been a twofold symbol. Life emerged from the water, and it cannot survive if it does not continue to be nourished by water. Fishermen respect the sea, for it provides them a living; desert nomads search the wilderness for the water necessary to feed their flocks and quench their thirst.

But death also lurks in the waters. The drought brings disaster to the nomad and the farmer; the storm threatens to flood out the land-dwellers and capsize the fisherman's frail craft. The water that gave life is also capable of taking it away. Men come and go in generations, they build bridges over the rivers, they run their water down great aqueducts, they erect cities and replace nature with technology. But the sea remains, unchanged, lapping the shorelines of our lives. And when we are gone and forgotten it remains what it always was.

Fire too carries life and death in itself. It brightens a winter room and provides warmth from the cold outside. It is an essential element in our cooking: no longer must we eat our meat raw. It is the source of our energy, the power behind our great advances. But like the sea it is a power often beyond our control. It eats up forests and makes the night sky bleed in agony. We die of cold from its absence and from burns in its excessive presence.

We have worshiped it as a god for its power, mystery and wonder, and we have cursed it as a demon and made it a symbol of hell for its pain and destructiveness. It both lights our darkness and darkens our life.

Oil is not as powerful a symbol as fire and water. But it has been almost universally used as a symbol for priesthood and the anointing of kings. Oil symbolizes something rich, pure and holy, something expensive. Many men use it to cleanse their bodies. Others use it to prepare their food. It is a base for expensive perfume, and it is often employed as a medicine for healing wounds.

Made history in Israel

These are the primary symbols of Christian initiation. Water and fire bring both life and death to man; oil anoints man and consecrates him, setting him aside for the high offices of priest and king. These symbols are all taken up into the experience of Israel. They play a vital role in Israel's encounter with God when they become embedded in history and help to mediate God's response to our dilemma, our vital question. Their meaning is purified and enriched in Israel's history and becomes less ambivalent.

God had freed Israel from the bondage of Egypt by leading her through the sea. The sea parted and the people walked on dry ground through its midst. Water became a primary remembrance of God's deliverance. Again, as the people were about to go into the land God had promised them, the river

Jordan which formed the boundary stopped flowing so that they could cross over.

But water could also be an instrument of God's anger and vengeance. The Israelites in their songs often saw God manifest in the storms that built up out at sea and then came raging onto the mainland. They told the story of how once upon a time God decided to destroy mankind for its wickedness. He caused it to rain for forty days and nights, creating a flood which destroyed all but one holy man and his family.

Water was also the source of life and nourishment. After the exodus the people wandered in the desert and God provided water from a rock for their thirst. God gives not only freedom but life itself. In the Hebrew story of the first man and woman there is a description of paradise. From this paradise of God ran four rivers which flowed out over the earth and watered it. Later in her history when Israel was destroyed and carried off to Babylon the prophet Ezekiel had a vision of the future temple which God would build in a restored Israel. Flowing from beneath the temple were four rivers, rivers flowing from God, rivers of regeneration and purification and nourishment.

Fire too was intimately associated with the exodus. God guided the people in a pillar of cloud by day and a pillar of fire by night. In Moses' first encounter with this saving God, he spoke from a burning bush. In both instances fire is a symbol of God's saving act.

Fire is also a symbol for purification and sacrifice. Like her neighbors, Israel offered sacrifice to her God through burnt offerings. But gradually through the teachings of the prophets it became plain that God most desired the sacrifice of loyalty and obedience to his Word.

The prophets often describe their encounter with God, using fire imagery. Isaiah tells how, when God called him to be a prophet, he protested that he was not worthy. An angel descended with a burning coal and placed it in Isaiah's mouth to purify him to speak the Word of God.

Like her neighbors, Israel consecrated places to God by pouring oil over them. Later, when she became a nation with a king, she anointed the king as a symbol of his office. As her days of glory faded into the past she looked forward to the great leader God had promised: the Messiah, God's anointed, the Christ in Greek. Anointing was thus a symbol of kingship, and it signaled God's approval upon a man for the office he was to fulfill. Anointing was a commission: it made a man king or priest and gave him a function and duty within the community. The king and the priest were dedicated to God and would serve as his ambassadors and instruments on earth.

Made flesh in Jesus

These great symbols, natural and historical, were gathered up in the Christian community and submerged in the reality of Jesus where they again were transformed and took on ever more meaning and power. Jesus at the beginning of his ministry presented himself to John the Baptist to be baptized. The Jewish ritual signified that a man was sorry for his sins and that he intended to change and amend his life.

Through his death and resurrection Jesus infuses new significance into baptism. Now it becomes a participation in Jesus' own death and resurrection. A man presents himself for baptism so that he may enter into the experience he has heard in the stories. He descends into the water and is submerged under the water which symbolizes death and the tomb. The old man dies and in his place rises a new man who has conquered death by being born into Jesus and putting on Jesus' experience of death and resurrection. The waters that take life also give life.

Israel had once passed through the water from slavery to freedom. God had chosen a people for his own and delivered them from their masters. Now in Jesus all can pass through the water from slavery to freedom. A new exodus is here, not only an exodus from physical chains and bonds, but a salvation from the slavery of divisiveness, sin and death. Rising from the watery grave, it is again Easter and we see now not with our old eyes but with the eyes of the risen Christ. We were not born for death, and now in baptism we have put on Jesus and his everlasting victory over death and destruction.

Before the sea parted, the people who stood on the Egyptian shore were merely a motley crew of escaped slaves. The people who stepped onto dry land after passing through the sea were a nation, bound together because of God's choice. No longer could they be strangers to one another: they were responsible for one another; their destiny was a common destiny.

The man who enters the font of baptism is an individual. Stepping out of the font afterward, he is part of a family, a new nation, a community, a Church. The early Christians saw themselves as the new Israel, called into being by God, incorporating all men. The Christian is not just an individual. In a real sense he is, first, part of a brotherhood, and he experiences God primarily in terms of his community. Baptism is the entrance into that community.

St. Paul speaks of baptism as "putting on Christ." When a man asks to be baptized he asks to participate in Jesus' experience. He wishes to live his life in a way similar to Jesus, to see the world as he saw it. In baptism the old self dies. The old life is renounced as the vision of Jesus is put on. Incorporated into the Lord the seeker enters into Christ's body. Paul calls the Church the body of Christ. Jesus is found today in the Church, in the group of people who have entered into his faith and his vision. There he lives and ministers today.

If in baptism we put on Christ, then in a very real sense we are what he is. He was God's Son, and by participation in him we too become sons of God. And if we are all sons of one Father in Jesus, then are we not brothers one to another? Jesus' preaching of the brotherhood of man is made real and concrete through baptism into his Church. We can no longer look out only for ourselves. A family or a nation places the obligation upon its members to live with one another, to help and care for one another. No longer can I see another man's sorrow and shrug it off because it does not affect me. It *does* affect me because that man and I are bound together and I have a responsibility toward him as I do toward a brother.

Finally baptism is a rebirth. It allows us a new start in life. If we are born into Christ in baptism, then the old man, the man of dissension, selfishness and greed dies. We have all sinned, done what we know is wrong. But in baptism our sins and failings are forgotten. They are washed away in the water and we are cleansed; freed from the chains of our past we can begin again. We can make the kind of life we want, the kind of life we have chosen in Jesus. No longer do we have failure, sin and death hanging over our heads, threatening our existence at every point. We have seen the sun rise over the tomb on Easter morning. A man clothed in brightness has pointed out the highway toward the city built on Love.

Encounter with God

In the sacrament we encounter Jesus at a particular point in our life. Receiving the sacrament we enter into his experience. But there is nothing magical. Christians grow old like all men and finally die. Nor are they exempt from the quarrels, divisions, strife and sin that inflict everyone. The Church's history shows she has always been composed of sinners. Baptism does not magically grant us immortality or free us from our often inadequate and sinful selves.

But neither is baptism a mere formality, like an initiation into a fraternity. In baptism a Christian truly is reborn. He is incorporated into Christ's body and forever belongs to Christ. But this gift of a new life and a new vision must be used. We receive the vision in baptism. But we spend the rest of our lives growing into this vision, conforming our will to Christ's will, our love to his.

In baptism we are given not only the gift of Christian experience but the power to utilize the gift and mold our lives in conformity with it. Many of us have felt the power present in a sunrise or sunset, the power of a poem, of a flower, of spring. In Christ man's natural symbols are gathered up and transformed. They become more gifted with meaning, more powerful, more able to transform us into Christ's image if we only open ourselves to them.

Jesus has given to his Church the sacraments as the very sources of his presence within her. They sustain and give life to the Church and she builds her whole existence around them: they are the air she breathes, the food she eats. As God became man in Jesus, so now through his death and resurrection all the universe is taken up into Jesus. Particularly in the Church's sacraments does he again become incarnate so that men might continue to meet and enter into his vision. Every time a sacrament is celebrated by the Church she has Jesus' promise that he will be present and that his power to transform will be working and given in this holy action. The sacrament of baptism bestows Christ's vision and the power to enter this vision.

But if the gift is to be assimilated so that it may transform us, we must cooperate in the process. Sacraments do not fail because they do not effect what they claim. They fail only because we do not allow their power to transform us.

For a Christian, water carries not only its natural and Old Testament meanings. Water is a symbol for Jesus Christ himself. He is the water that truly quenches our thirst for knowledge. He is the water able to cleanse us from our wrongs, our selfishness, our fears, our sins. His is the healing water with the power to bring us through the waters of death, to heal our wounds, to give sight to us who were blind.

He is also our light, our fire, our candle. St. John calls him the light of the world. The light came into the darkness, but the darkness did not understand it. Nor could the darkness overcome it. The light illumines every man who comes into the world.

Every year as Christians celebrate the great feast of Easter, an Easter fire is kindled before the Church. The fire is a symbol for Jesus and his victory over the darkness of the grave. All take their candle and light it from the fire. Then everyone proceeds into the darkened church. Dark death is overcome as the light spreads from candle to candle, from Christian to Christian. Christ's light is ablaze in hundreds of candles; the one man who conquered death has made it possible for the whole world to walk in his light, to carry his light into the darkness of their lives and to dispel that darkness.

The early Christians celebrated baptism during the Easter Vigil. On the night when Christ broke the bonds of death they relived that event in baptism. Before the great Easter candle, the pillar of cloud and fire for the new Israel, the convert passed through the waters of death and arose to life in Christ. He was then given a new white robe as a sign of his new purity and innocence. Then a candle was presented to him. Lit from the paschal candle, it was a sign for Christ's light now in him. Finally he was anointed with oil to signify his entrance into Jesus' kingship and priesthood.

Christian mission

Oil was used in Israel in the ceremonies for coronation and the ordination of priests. Jesus was the true king, not only of Israel but of all men. He was the true priest, for he mediated between God and man. The baptized enters into Christ and assumes his mission and ministry. Christians are a royal people, God's chosen people, a priestly people. It is their ministry to unite the world, to build a community of love in the community of man.

Through the anointing with holy oil Christians are ordained and receive a mission to carry Christ's light to the rest of mankind. They must minister to their fellow man, teach him the good news, heal his wounds and quarrels, free him from physical and spiritual bondage, and bring him out of darkness into light.

Such was the sacrament of baptism in the earliest days of the Church. At first all Christian converts were adults. But soon these Christians had children. A problem arose whether the children should be baptized immediately or should grow up and then ask to be baptized. The community decided that their children should be baptized. They could not make a decision for the faith as an adult could, but they were born into a Christian home and their parents would raise them in the faith. So the body of Christ now included children who could grow up physically and spiritually in that body. As Europe became Christian, soon most baptisms were of children, and it remains so today.

But a child could not be expected to carry on his Christian mission and ministry. He is a passive Christian, receiving rather than giving. So as infant baptism became more prominent, the ceremony of anointing was separated from it.

This ceremony, which in the earliest days was a part of baptism, symbolized the Christian's witness and ministry to all men. Now it was postponed until the child had grown into adulthood and was ready to undertake his duty to witness. It became the sacrament of Christian maturity and is known as confirmation. Confirmation today is thought of by most Christians as a separate sacrament. But its purpose, the commissioning of the Christian to show his faith to the world in his life and actions, is really only the completion of what was begun in baptism. The two sacraments must be seen together.

Every sacrament exists not only so that a man may experience Jesus but also so that he may carry the fruits of that experience with him into the world. Christians live for other men, not solely for themselves. Their model is a man who laid down his life for his friends.

Significant texts on baptism are found in Matthew 3, John 3:1-21, John 4:1-42, and Colossians 2:6-17.

 The Church Praying

From the Baptismal Liturgy

Father, you give us grace through sacramental signs,
    which tell us of the wonders of your unseen
                    power.
In baptism we use your gift of water,
    which you have made a rich symbol of the grace
        you give us in this sacrament.
At the very dawn of creation your Spirit breathed
                on the waters,
    making them the wellspring of all holiness.
The waters of the great flood you made a sign of
                the waters
    of baptism, that made an end of sin
        and a new beginning of goodness.
Through the waters of the Red Sea you led Israel
            out of slavery,
    to be an image of God's holy people,
        set free from sin by baptism.
In the waters of the Jordan your Son was baptized
                by John
    and anointed with the Spirit.
Your Son willed that water and blood should flow
                from his side
    as he hung upon the cross.

After his resurrection he told his disciples:
    "Go out and teach all nations, baptizing them
    in the name of the Father and of the Son and of
            the Holy Spirit."
Father, look now with love upon your Church,
    and unseal for her the fountain of baptism.
By the power of the Spirit give to the water of this
            fount
    the grace of your Son.
You created man in your own likeness: cleanse
            him from sin
    in a new birth to innocence by water and the
            Spirit.

We ask you, Father, with your Son to send the
Holy Spirit upon the water of this fount. May all
who are buried with Christ in the death of baptism
rise also with him to newness of life. Amen.

8

Sacrament of Christian Nourishment and Growth—Eucharist

The gift of new life and vision which Christians receive in baptism and confirmation must be nourished if it is to grow and transform us. Just as our bodies need physical nourishment to grow to adulthood, so we need spiritual nourishment as well. The Mass or eucharist is the source of this nourishment.

Meal and Word

The eucharist is built upon three symbols: word, wine and bread. Bread and wine, the fundamental foods of many peoples, symbolize food and drink. Bread is the mainstay for many people for whom meat is a luxury. It keeps them alive: without it they would die. It does not occupy such a central place in our own diet, but memories of bread's importance linger in proverbs such as: "Bread is the staff of life."

Wine too in many cultures assumes an importance that it does not have for us. It forms the normal dinner drink, but it also carries festive connotations. Being alcoholic, it lifts the spirits, makes conversation easier, and adds zest to the meal. It has the ability to enliven an otherwise ordinary meal; it is a symbol for rejoicing and feasting.

The meal itself has great significance for man. A true meal is not just a means of nourishing the body. Meals are to be savored and enjoyed. They provide relaxation and enjoyment after a day's work. Mealtime is a time set aside to enjoy the earth's food and to share the companionship of others close to us. We share ourselves with one another in conversation, fellowship and gentle humor. Our true model for a meal should be a family-style Thanksgiving dinner when the meal becomes an event rather than the quick bite grabbed or the drab fare gulped to stay alive.

The third eucharistic symbol is the word. Consider the miracle of the word. Words make us men, different from all other animals. We are animals who think and believe and hold ideas we are willing to die for: all because of the word's power.

The power of the word can heal a breach between men: "Forgive me, I'm sorry." It can make two people one: "I love you." It can carry us by images, stories and poems to places we have never been. Through slander and anger it can destroy our society with one another. Through philosophy and science it makes possible those wonders that our ancestors scarcely dreamed of. Such is the power of the word.

Remembering in Israel

Israel recognized the power of the word, but for Israel the word was primarily God's Word. In the beginning God had but to speak a word and the universe came into being. God's Word was in the Law which he made with Israel. He promised to make them a nation if they kept his Word. And later his Word blazed forth from the prophets as they brought God's judgment upon a people who had ceased to heed the Word. In her wisdom literature Israel studied God's purpose in history to find his Word for the living of their lives. They saw that God's wisdom comes forth from him to enlighten men in his ways.

But in addition to God's Word Israel was diligent in remembering his deeds which had brought her into existence. Each year she celebrated the feast of Passover in memory of her passing over from the bondage of Egypt into her freedom as God's people. She ate unleavened bread in remembrance of the flight when her ancestors had to eat unleavened bread because they could not stay in one place long enough to bake leavened bread.

The family ate a lamb in remembrance of the lamb's blood which the Israelites had splashed over their doorways so that God would pass over their houses on the night he struck dead the firstborn of the Egyptians. Israel was saved by that lamb's blood.

And she drank wine in celebration and thanksgiving for what God had done for her, bringing her out of slavery and giving her a land of her own. Through the ritual meal Israel relived down through the centuries her exodus. She made it present again each year in the songs, stories and above all in the eating of the meal itself.

Ritual is a play, a game. We open ourselves as we do in a game. We enter into the events we are celebrating; we put them on, and for the duration all sense of daily time disappears. When we play a game we are not aware of time's passing. Our imagination takes over and for a moment we escape the clock and our present surroundings. We enter another world, a sacred timeless world. We are like little children playing at being grown up—for the duration of the game we are grown up. In ritual, present time disappears and we participate in the original event. We put on the vision our ancestors had and we rejoice that God has delivered us. In acting out the sacred game the past becomes alive for us and we are united with those men of long ago. We bring their experience to life in our own lives.

The Passover of Jesus

The night before he died Jesus celebrated the Passover meal with his disciples. But in doing so he gave the meal a new meaning so that when in the future his disciples celebrated this meal they would primarily remember Jesus rather than the old exodus.

Jesus took bread into his hands, and when he had given thanks to God he broke it and gave it to his disciples, saying, "Take and eat. This is my body." When supper was over he took the cup of wine. Again giving thanks he blessed the cup and passed it to his disciples, saying, "Take and drink. This is my blood, which shall be shed for all men. Do this in memory of me."

Bread, the staff of life, our bodily food, is taken up by Jesus and made into his body—given to us as food so that we might grow into him. The festive wine becomes his blood shed on the cross—now made the drink that unites us to him. This simple action becomes the Christian Passover—our remembrance of Jesus' work. How God himself became a man and died on a cross so that all men might live—this is what we remember. We remember a new exodus from sin and death into everlasting life. We celebrate a new freedom as sons of God.

This simple communion makes present for us the act of our salvation. We remember Jesus, his death and resurrection, and through the holy game of the meal, Jesus in the form of bread and wine gives himself up for us. He becomes food which nourishes us and brings us into eternal life. In the mystery of this celebration we are present on the hill of crucifixion and before the tomb on Easter morning. Time stops, and for the duration of the rite we live at the same time as the original events. Just as once on the cross, so now Jesus gives himself so that men might not die but live.

Christian eucharist

At first the eucharist was celebrated in homes, but as Christians were driven out of the synagogues, and as the Christian communities became larger, they began meeting before dawn on Sunday to celebrate the Lord's resurrection. They adopted the first part of the service from the synagogue: it consisted of prayers, songs and readings from the Scriptures. Then they celebrated the eucharistic meal. So arose the basic form of Christian service still used today.

The liturgy of the Word as the first part of the Mass is called is a celebration of the works of God through prayers, songs and readings. From the beginning Christians have seen Jesus as God's Word to man. Jesus is the perfect expression of man: in this man God has given all men an example and exemplar. If we are distinguished from the animals because of our words, then it is only natural that God should communicate himself to us in the form of the Word which was Jesus.

God is encountered today primarily through his sacraments: creation made transparent to let him shine through into our lives. But the sacramental symbol is never alone: it is always made fully human through God's accompanying Word. Christianity's stumbling block is that God has taken upon himself his creation in order to express himself. Water, bread and wine fully communicate God to man. The God who went so far as to become man also deigns to use human language to express himself. Human speech has been made divine, inadequate as it is. Sacraments are not speechless. They communicate through the senses, but through the Word they reach the core of our humanity also.

Christ's presence among us

Christians have often talked of the eucharist as a presence of Christ among his people. And his presence is very manifest in every celebration of the Mass. First, as Jesus promised, he is present whenever two or three are gathered together in his name. His Church is his very body. He is present also when his story and his message are proclaimed.

The Scriptures are truly God's Word, somehow contained in our fragile words. When the message is proclaimed and heard among men, then Jesus, who is the Word of God, is present.

Christ is also present in the person of the priest or minister. The priest assumes the role that Christ performed at the Last Supper. He celebrates the eucharist in Christ's name. In the ritual action he ceases to be an individual. He now acts in the name of his Lord who is present to the community through this man. Just as God chose incredibly to become a man to reach men, so now he uses the person of the priest to be present to his people.

Then Christ is present in the bread and wine. Christians believe that in the mystery of this sacrament the bread and the wine truly become the body and blood of Jesus, given to men for their nourishment and salvation. He is present in the bread and wine without it seeming to be any less bread and wine than before. Throughout the centuries theologians have attempted to understand more profoundly this mystery and they have developed complex and elaborate theologies to aid in penetrating the mystery. But no matter how brilliant the insight, the mystery remains, and it remains at the center of Christian faith: our food and drink as long as we remain upon this earth. No Christian can explain it, but he firmly believes in Jesus' real presence in the eucharist. As Jesus was truly God without damage to his humanity, so in this sacrament he is truly present in his body and blood without the elements of bread and wine being destroyed.

The eucharist is the source and nourishment for Christian experience. Its celebration makes men one in their communion with Christ. As the wheat scattered on the hillsides was made one in the bread, so men scattered over the earth are brought into one through the bread of Jesus broken so that all men might be united in him and with one another.

In the eucharist we enter most closely into relationship with Christ as we hear his Word, partake of his body and blood, and join in union with our brothers to praise our Father. Strengthened by this communion we again go out into the world to bring men good news. We come together to renew and strengthen our faith so that we may continue our mission to the world. At the end of Mass the priest says, "The Mass is ended. Go forth to love and serve the Lord." To which every Christian replies: "Thanks be to God" both now and forever.

Important biblical texts concerning the eucharist are found in Mark 14:12-31, 1 Corinthians 11:17-34, and especially John 6.

 The Church Praying

From the Eucharistic Liturgy

Priest: *Father, it is our duty and our salvation,*
           always and everywhere
           to give you thanks
           through your beloved Son, Jesus Christ.

He is the Word through whom you made
  the universe,
the Savior you sent to redeem us.
By the power of the Holy Spirit
he took flesh and was born of the Virgin
  Mary.
For our sake he opened his arms on the
  cross;
he put an end to death
and revealed the resurrection.
In this he fulfilled your will
and won for you a holy people.

And so we join with the angels and the
  saints
in proclaiming your glory as we say:

People: Holy, holy, holy Lord, God of power and
            might,
          Heaven and earth are full of your glory.
          Hosanna in the highest.
          Blessed is he who comes in the name of
            the Lord.
          Hosanna in the highest.

Priest: Lord, you are holy indeed,
          the fountain of all holiness.
          Let your Spirit come upon these gifts to
            make them holy,
          so that they may become for us
          the body and blood of our Lord, Jesus
            Christ.

          Before he was given up to death,
          a death he freely accepted,

he took bread and gave you thanks.
He broke the bread,
gave it to his disciples, and said:
Take this, all of you, and eat it:
this is my body which will be given up for
   you.
When supper was ended, he took the cup.
Again he gave you thanks and praise,
gave the cup to his disciples, and said:
Take this, all of you, and drink from it:
this is the cup of my blood,
the blood of the new and everlasting
   covenant.
It will be shed for you and for all men
so that sins may be forgiven.
Do this in memory of me.
Let us proclaim the mystery of faith:

People: *Christ has died,*
         Christ is risen,
         Christ will come again.

Priest: *In memory of his death and resurrection,*
         we offer you, Father, this life-giving bread,
         this saving cup.
         We thank you for counting us worthy
         to stand in your presence and serve you.

         May all of us who share in the body and
            blood of Christ
         be brought together in unity by the Holy
            Spirit.

         Lord, remember your Church throughout
            the world;

make us grow in love,
together with our Pope,
our bishop, and all the clergy.

Remember our brothers and sisters
who have gone to their rest
in the hope of rising again;
bring them and all the departed
into the light of your presence.

Have mercy on us all;
make us worthy to share eternal life
with Mary, the virgin mother of God,
with the apostles,
and with all the saints who have done your
    will throughout the ages.
May we praise you in union with them,
and give you glory
through your Son, Jesus Christ.

Through him,
with him,
in him,
in the unity of the Holy Spirit,
all glory and honor is yours,
almighty Father, for ever and ever.
                                    Amen.

Part IV
The Ethics of
Christianity

9

The Wonder and Mystery of Man

We have been talking about the Christian transformation of man in baptism and the eucharist. It is now time to ask what man is. Is he basically good or evil?

The human animal

What is man? He is an animal: the only one who talks or thinks. He is a tool maker, a builder, a painter. And in this he is unique. But he is also unique as the animal who kills for the joy of killing. He can at one time be higher than any other animal and at another be more beastly and willingly cruel than any other creature. He is the only animal who laughs or smiles and the only animal who can destroy others merely by speaking.

He can improve himself or degrade himself. No one would tell a dog to act like a dog—the animal can do nothing else. But should a man act inappropriately, he will be told to act like a man. Man has the freedom to become better, an angel, or worse, a beast. He has the genius to build a hydrogen bomb and the depravity to explode one.

"Many awesome things there be under the sun, but none as awesome as man," says Sophocles. He

87

is truly a marvel, the only creature who wonders. Only man knows of a world besides the external one: a world within himself as seemingly vast, deep and incomprehensible as the external universe of stars.

Man is torn between two poles: himself and others. Shall he escape the mob, be independent, go off on his own? Or should he join with other men in building a society? Others impede his freedom and hurt him, but can he afford to cut himself off from their support, their companionship, their love?

Israel and social man

Israel found the answer to the question of man at her very beginning. She was a society of free men. She was not a tyranny where all bow their will to the whim of the tyrant, but neither was she an anarchy where no man is his brother's keeper. Each man is part of the whole, each supports the society and in turn is supported.

Israel experienced God acting to build a society of men. She learned to rely upon and even need the society of men. Man can only be man within a society: one man alone can not exist. God encounters Israel through society and history: he makes a covenant with a people, he establishes a nation, he sets up a monarchy to lead the nation, and when the society fails to live up to the covenant he sends individual prophets who give their lives to rescue the people and return them to God. God is revealed through politics, and the Israelite found his true identity as part of a people that God had chosen and created. He found the deepest meaning

of his life as he relived year after year the Passover
from slavery into freedom, and he shared that experience as part of a group of men with a common
tradition.

Israel's story chronicles God's founding of a nation. But although men may desire to live together
in society and want to dwell in peace, there is a
disease which brings to nothing all our attempts:
the disease of sin.

A hermit would not encounter sin. Assuming he
could go about his life, scraping together a sub-
sistence, eventually he would die of some natural
cause or accident. But completely alone and never
knowing another human being, he would live much
as a cow—forging for food, his only care to escape
destruction one day at a time, no thought because
no language, his only emotions satisfaction or pain,
his only hurts physical. He would exist and he
would die and there would be an end of him.

But could such a being be a man? No. A man
talks and thinks, remembers and laughs. But to do
any of these things he must have fellows, and he
must get along with them and live in peace.

The blessing of law

It does not seem a very difficult thing to live
in peace. All we need are a few rules, some conventions, a minimum of agreement and a little good
will. On Mount Sinai God provided Israel with such
a law. It guarded against division and strife arising
within the society, offering ten simple rules designed
to prevent sin. Honor your elders. Do not steal.
Do not kill. Do not commit adultery. Do not bear
false witness against your neighbor. Do not envy

your neighbor. Worship the Lord as your only God. Do not worship false gods. Do not take the Lord's name lightly. Reserve one day a week to remember God.

There is nothing startling or unexpected in these ten commandments. Most of them form the basis for any cooperative living among men. Only the commands concerning God are unique to Israel. But there lies the secret to peace. Only under God can man be in harmony. When we place ourself in God's seat, society's fabric is stretched and torn. With no God, man in his pride becomes a god and arrogates to himself the privilege of abrogating the other commands. The proud man is above the law: he feels society should center around him.

Israel was taught that society can only work when it revolves not around man or a group of men but God. When God is not honored a false god is: the god of man's pride, the fateful cruel god of nature and her laws, the god of wealth and worldly success. Israel in her history followed all these gods, and because she did so she fell, crushed under her own sins.

The curse of law

But let us not stand on a peak and judge Israel. Let us take the commandments upon ourselves. They are quite simple and easy to understand. They are reasonable and no man would be unwilling to subscribe to them. Nor do they seem difficult to keep. With a little good will on the part of all we could make Israel's covenant a reality in our world.

But when we attempt to live seriously by these simple commands we begin to see the grave difficulty involved. They are broken constantly, and not only by the undesirable element of society. We break them continually ourselves. We may manage for a few days and congratulate ourselves. But what of the couple next door? You heard the quarrel they had last night until two in the morning, and you just have to tell someone about it. Or you become angry at your son because he left his tricycle in the drive again. Sure you had a right to become angry—but *that* angry? Because you had a rough day at work, does your little boy deserve the bile you have accumulated during the day? No one sets out to violate the society's bans on adultery. But before we know it we are seeing another man or woman, and we are hopelessly entangled in an affair. We now see the impossibility of conforming to the law of righteousness.

The harmonious society that the commandments were meant to produce never materializes. These ten guides toward good living given us by God come to be condemning judges of our behavior. Instead of leading us to happiness they accuse us of our failure. St. Paul goes so far as to say that they bring sin into the world because they hold up a mirror showing how far we have strayed from God and his ways. Before the law we lived in ignorance, but through the law we have seen the truth, and we cannot possibly live the truth. The more we try to succeed the greater our failure. The law provided for our improvement has only thrown into relief our meanness and wretchedness.

We know the good, we want to do the good, but

we always fail to accomplish the good. We build a civilization, a perfect city, but there is a crack in the foundation. The worm eats away inside our noblest action and eventually brings it to nothing. We are doomed to failure. We build utopias and the very word tells us of our failure, for "u-topia" means "no-place." It cannot exist here in spite of its simplicity.

St. Paul knew acutely our dilemma which later theologians have called "original sin." Our imperfection accuses us and declares that we are not what we should be. Something has gone awry, and Paul lays the blame for this original sin upon man himself. For God is righteous and just—such is the two thousand year experience of Israel. The fault cannot be with him who detests evil and calls for its defeat. If not God, then we must acknowledge ourselves as somehow guilty. Nor is it an accidental defect: we are not automatons but free and responsible beings, and if we would live up to our responsibility then we must shoulder the sin, the disease, which has come to be part of being human.

Israel disobeyed the law and the law condemned her sin. How can man be reconciled, how can we be brought together with ourselves, our brothers and God? The law demonstrates our helplessness; we are left without hope of reconciliation and peace.

A faithful servant

What if one man in his life should be able to fulfill the law? We are inclined to say he would be a saint, a great leader of men. He would be admired, respected, even worshiped. But we must remember that he would have to live his life without sin in the depths of a world torn apart by sin. He would be a saint among sinners.

When we attempt to change ourselves, one of the first difficulties we encounter is our friends. The worst enemies of the man who gives up smoking are his smoking friends. They constantly remind him of cigarettes and unwittingly tempt him by smoking in his presence. Sometimes they even become indignant that he has stopped smoking because they see it as a judgment upon themselves.

How easy it would be to be sinless in a sinless society. But every time I attempt to live the law I am hurt by other men's sinfulness. The prophet Isaiah envisioned an Israel without sin, an Israel conforming to God. In a series of beautiful songs he told of such a faithful servant of God. He imagined Israel as an individual and the other nations as Israel's fellow men. The servant Israel led a blameless life. But because of her obedience and holiness she is hated by her fellows and put to death. She seems weak and ugly to look at; she is a laughingstock. The scorning nations spit upon her. Such is the lot of the sinless in a sinful world.

Healed by his stripes

Isaiah's songs of the sinless Israel were not fulfilled. However in Jesus the world found a sinless man—a man without blame, totally obedient to God. And the reward of such sinlessness was rejection by his fellow men. Our sin cannot stand holiness: something inside us relishes the downfall of a good man. Jesus' holiness was rewarded by a cross and death.

But in Jesus' life the old covenant had been lived and given flesh. Although not sinful, he had suffered death, the consequence of sin. But God refused to let sinful man prevail. Taking the "no" of Jesus' condemnation by man, he answered it with an eternal "yes" through the resurrection. Man had committed the most heinous sin possible: killing an innocent man. God responded by turning that crime into a victory and a triumph. The worst man could do was answered by the greatest God could do: Jesus conquered death and destroyed sin. He had lived a life free of sin and had merited eternal life with God. He had replaced Israel and had become God's true servant.

In Israel many men had represented one entity: in Jesus one man comes to represent all men. Through baptism into him we are made sinless and righteous. We do not deserve this favor, nor can we earn it. It is a gift of God. We stand in the right even though we have done the wrong. We are sinless even though we have sinned.

The power in Jesus' victory enables us to conquer sin in our own lives. We stand in his body and model ourselves upon him in the assurance that his victory is our victory and that in him we too can be sinless because we share his power over sin and death. The victory has already been accomplished in Jesus. All that remains is its realization in our own lives.

In Christ's body a new society is formed, freed from the bondage of sin and death. But although there is the power and the possibility of sanctity, there is also the acknowledgment that baptism does not entirely destroy the old man. If it did we would not be free: we would be determined toward holiness after baptism just as we were determined toward sin before. Sin still breaks out in the community of the saved, but it can never prevail—its death is already present.

The Church as Christ's body is sinless, but inasmuch as she is still in the world and composed of sinful men she is also sinful. She is the new Israel. The old Israel had a law which laid out the conditions for a peaceful and happy society. The new Israel has in the person of her Lord already fulfilled the law: peace and happiness are at hand. She needs to win no victory; she needs only make actual its results in her life. She is a bride in pilgrimage to her groom, and at the same time she is already there at his side.

The ten commandments are found in Deuteronomy 5.

The Song of the Suffering Servant is in Isaiah 52:13-53:12.

Paul speaks of Jesus and the law in Romans 5—7.

10

The Christian's Own Story

"Free at last"

Freedom from sin and death is the beginning of Christian life, not its end. In baptism man is made into Christ and has conquered. But how is he to live? What makes Christian existence different?

There is nothing very new in Christian ethics: no secret rule Christians follow unknown to other men. The difference is not in rules and law but in outlook and attitude.

Paul found that Jewish law only served to make man aware of his sin. This awareness would then lead to despair—for how could man possibly avoid sin and achieve peace with his fellows and God? The Christian knows that he too is sinful but that in spite of his sin he is freed from it through Jesus. Thus the Christian's life becomes an exploration of his new freedom, and with the power he receives from Jesus in baptism and the eucharist he breaks the actual bondage of sin in his own life.

The Christian's life is a reflection upon and a variation of Jesus' story. He appropriates into his own life the freedom and power of Jesus over sin

and death. And if this experience should become
central, then his life will speak of the Jesus-experi-
ence to all he meets. The more he enters into
Jesus' vision, the more his life will tell a story
similar to that of Jesus.

The Christian makes real in his own life the love
for God and for all men which Jesus had. He is able
to forgive other people when they wrong him; he
becomes strong enough to return love for hate,
right for wrong. He sees the necessity of love and
that love must be spent—it cannot be hoarded. So
he makes service real in his life and gives love
flesh.

Cross and glory

But if a Christian would live a Christ-life, can its
reward be any different than that of the cross? The
world is still sinful and Christian life is bound to
bring some form of suffering. Perhaps the cross
tasks the form of disease, or failure, or the loss of
friends. Although he cannot escape sin and suffering, yet the Christian knows that suffering is not
final; it cannot destroy him.

The cross is his victory: Christian suffering shows
others the power of Jesus to transform and redeem
man's sinful condition. Suffering, accepted in the
faith that it cannot kill but has already met its
defeat in the cross, tells the world a much different
story than suffering given in to, despaired over and
thought hopeless.

During the centuries Christians have made Jesus
clearly visible in their lives. These men and women

were truly other Christs, living Jesus' story in their own culture and age. And the Church has held these men and women up to other Christians for imitation. What does it mean to be a Christian? Consider Christ's saints.

A short glance at the infinite variety of saints convinces anyone of the freedom within the vision of Jesus. Francis of Assisi gave up everything—family, wealth, title—to follow Jesus as a pauper. Thomas More was chancellor of England under Henry VIII, yet he preferred to lose his position and finally his life rather than compromise his vision of Jesus. Isaac Jogues, a missionary to the American Indians, suffered cruel tortures at their hands willingly, hoping to bring them his vision of Jesus. Thomas Aquinas, Christ's scholar, at the time when the philosophy of Aristotle threatened Christian faith, brought the principles of Aristotelianism into the service of the faith. All for the greater glory of God!

Conscience's spur

Granted that every Christian should show forth Christ in his life, how can he achieve this goal in the concrete experiences of daily living? How can he decide whether one course of action is better than another?

The source of our decision-making process is that mysterious entity called a conscience. Whenever confronted with a major decision involving right and wrong, we supposedly follow this conscience. "Let your conscience be your guide." A Christian can do no better.

But what is a conscience? Is it always right? Two mothers of small children become pregnant again. One mother terminates her pregnancy while the other mother, although her family is big enough already, has her baby because she cannot in conscience have an abortion. Is each woman right? Is one conscience as good as another? Is what a man does indifferent so long as he thinks it is right? Hitler believed he was right and few would want to have seen him succeed.

Conscience is a person's sense of right and wrong. When confronted by a decision I do not decide on a mere whim. I have some idea whether a course of action is right or wrong, good or evil. I also wish to take account of my action's consequences.

Take a simple example: I am hungry and a basket of green apples lies before me. Should I eat them or not? A little boy might decide to eat them. But I as an adult would probably forego the pleasure. Foreseeing the stomach ache, I would consider it wrong to satisfy my hunger in this way. And the little boy, after he has suffered from the apples, would come to see the problem as I do: the immediate pleasure and good of eating the apples is not worth the misery and pain of the nausea.

This trivial example shows in part how conscience develops. It is not built into us—it grows and matures. Indeed most of our education consists in conscience development. It converts us from savages into civilized men: we do not kill each other over a slight misunderstanding, we do not cheat, we believe in respect, trust and fairness rather than chicanery, scheming and thievery, we do not eat green apples.

We are not born with an already-formed conscience, only with the capacity to develop one. The baby, cute as he is, is totally self-centered and demanding. But his education begins almost immediately: he must learn to control his urges to wet his diaper, he must learn to eat at certain times rather than when he happens to get hungry. He must learn the value of property—he cannot play with his mother's china. He must control his anger—he can not hit his sister every time he feels like it. And so it goes throughout his life.

Man has many teachers: his parents most importantly. But also his culture: children in America soon learn that it is not good to get dirty, while mothers elsewhere may not be concerned about cleanliness at all. A child's peers greatly influence his conscience. When the child is old enough we put him into a school which teaches him how to get along in society. His mind is filled with the knowledge he will need to function in his society, and his behavior is changed and modified so that he will fit into society.

Finally, religion plays an important role: we are taught that some things are good and others evil because God has said so. If a child wishes to act in the face of the disapproval of his parents, his friends, his teachers and God himself, he weighs the situation and probably decides that although it would be very gratifying to belt his sister in the mouth, it would also produce some very ungratifying side-effects far outweighing the initial pleasure.

Considering again the two pregnant mothers we see that there are many variations of conscience possible within a society, and of course there are many differences between various societies. Two people may not assimilate the culture's taboos against certain behavior to the same extent. Or they may emerge with different consciences because of a difference in their parents' outlook or their religious affiliation. When the conscience-building process fails, another variation, the criminal or deviate, results.

Is there any element of this fluid conscience that rises above happenstance? Is our conscience simply an accident decreed by upbringing, environment and genes? Are we ultimately slaves to this censor in our brain?

The God of conscience

Israel found that conscience need not be an arbitrary whim fate plays upon us. It should be directed by something larger than ourselves, our parents, or our society. The source and molder of conscience should be God, for only he can reveal to us the truth. Israel read her history as a slow education of her conscience by God. She believed there was progress: while once it was acceptable to wipe out an enemy down to the last woman and child, Israel later realized that such an action was not really consonant with the reality God had revealed to her.

God's law showed a path between the anarchy of relativism where every man is his own law and the suffocation of tyranny where one man decides the law for all. God's law was a freeing experience because it provided the structures within which a society could live in peace and harmony.

But Israel's law too became a tyranny. Unable to hold to its spirit, men degraded its observance into a formalism: they obeyed the letter and thought that sufficient. Law became an end rather than a means.

Troubler of the complacent

Jesus is no destroyer of Israel's law. True, he replaces it, but he did so not by abolition but by fulfillment. Men too easily gloat in self-satisfaction. If I have managed to keep the Sabbath holy, if I have paid my respects to God, if I have not cheated on my neighbor, then I can sit down with a certain satisfaction. I have fulfilled my duty. God is duly appeased.

"If you should think evil against a man in your mind, then you have as well as killed him in the flesh." These words shake us out of our complacency. *God* is the fulfillment of the law. Law is not an end in itself; it is a beginning.

Israel's conscience had become static. It was formed and then simply referred to in determining how to act. Make the law your conscience, then regulate your actions accordingly. How many of us still think this way? We know right from wrong; we are constructive, law-abiding members of society; our faults are minor and forgivable.

Jesus refused to accept this complacence. The

holiness of God goes far beyond the minimalism of the law. He accused the Israelites of a dead conscience. As long as we live we must strive toward God and his holiness. Our call is not to the security *and* the tyranny of a static conscience. We must expand our vision and be free of all tyranny.

Conscience may be wrong; it will always be imperfect. In Jesus we have a model and a vision of God which cannot be minimalized. We need no law because in him we are already just. But we do have his call to go continually beyond ourselves. And his teachings serve as guideposts along our way. Love one another as you love yourself. Return love for hatred. Let forgiveness replace vengeance. Be guided by charity rather than justice. These are not laws but models which found their perfect expression in Jesus' life.

A Christian is free from the tyranny of conscience. The law had said: Do this and live. Jesus says: Live and do this. We are not justified by our conscience; we are justified by God. Nor are we tied to our conscience: often it should be corrected through a deeper understanding of Jesus.

Conscience continues to be formed every day of our life—through God's Word in Holy Scripture, through the teachings of the Christian community, through encyclicals (official teachings of the pope in the name of the entire Church), through our family and friends, and, most important through prayer.

We cannot abdicate our freedom—we must follow God's voice in our conscience, even if it be against the advice of parents, country, friends or pope. If we are open to advice and change, if we are sincere in seeking God's will, then we can only follow God; anything else is tyranny and slavery. He is our only judge and corrector; we are under no law and will be judged only by God's mercy seen in Jesus Christ.

Christian behavior is not following rules. Christians are not a people of the law. They cannot go through life following the laws and keeping their noses clean. If we are made righteous because we stand in Jesus, if we are sons of God because he was God's Son, then our life must model his. As sons, Christians are responsible for their brothers. We are not called to obey some law but to freely give ourselves to our fellow man. We are called to show our freedom in action.

Mercy tempers justice in our lives. If a brother in need asks for money, it is justice to give him what he needs and it is mercy to give him more. It is justice to see that no man suffers because of his color; it is love and mercy to welcome him as a brother. It is justice to repay a wrong with punishment; it is mercy to forgive. If we would stand in Jesus, then we must act like Jesus: love knows no limit.

"Sleepers, awake!"

One of the earliest Christian hymns had a phrase concerning "sleepers who wake from the dark." Christians are men who have awakened from the sleep of inaction and indifference. In Jesus we see what it means to be truly alive. Life is only alive when it is motivated by love. Selfishness is another word for death. Life means other people and it means living for others.

We wake up to the needs of our fellow men: first their physical needs of clothing, health and food, then their needs of education, cultural enrichment and spiritual happiness. We meet these needs because we are thankful: our need for meaning has been met in Jesus Christ. And the only adequate response we can make consists in sharing our joy with others.

We wake to the needs of our country. We teach, we heal, we become a public servant. Of course not all can act in such a capacity. But all citizens share the responsibility to bring about conditions of peace and harmony. As Christians we awake from our lethargy. We take our citizenship seriously. We exercise our right to vote with intelligence. We participate in the formation of public policy. We voice our opinion on issues.

We wake to the needs of mankind. World peace remains a mere dream unless men dedicate themselves to concrete action. We cannot shrug off responsibility if we would be alive. The fight against disease requires our support, through political action, or through economic support of various agencies, or through a scientific career.

We wake to the needs of the Christian community. We may educate children in the faith, visit sick members of the community, or help in a soup kitchen which feeds derelict men. We can help financially to support the Church's mission of good news. We could devote our lives to some form of Christian ministry. We can offer our talents to help in the celebration of the liturgy.

These are only a very few of the possible extensions of Christ's vision and action into the world. No one can hope to do more than a little. Some are called to do more, some less. But we all have a freedom to choose to live our life, not to let our life live us. Our life is free, a gift, not dictated by fate or chance. We are commissioned to make of our life a story, a song: a story that speaks of what we believe in, a song of life's meaning, of a purpose to living. If our story does not betray our vision, then Jesus is made flesh once more on this earth: another particle of creation is lifted up into God and made divine.

> *The most famous passage of Jesus' teaching is the Sermon on the Mount in Matthew 5—7.*
>
> *Paul explains to the Romans how a Christian should act in Romans 12— 15:13.*
>
> *John places in Jesus' mouth one of the most beautiful prayers for the care of his followers in John 17.*

 The Church Praying

A Christian Examination of Conscience

We can be sure we are in God only when we are living the same kind of life as Christ lived (1 John 2:5).

A young man once asked Jesus, "Master, what must I do?" And Jesus replied, "What does the law say?" The youth answered, "You must love the Lord your God with all your heart, soul, strength and mind, and your neighbor as yourself." "Do this," said Jesus (Luke 10:25-28).

A Christian deepens his love of God:

- *through a life nourished by deep and inner prayer which feeds on the prayer life of the Church herself.*
- *through frequent meditation on God's Word in Scripture.*
- *through participation in Christ's sacraments where the Christian enters more deeply into the vision of Jesus.*
- *by celebrating each Sunday as the day of the Lord and joining with fellow Christians in the eucharist on that day and on other important feast days.*
- *through a spirit of sacrifice and self-denial by which we learn to control our passions and become less self-centered.*

Christian love for the neighbor means:

- *I can exclude no one from universal brotherly love.*
- *I will live more for others than for myself.*
- *I am faithful to my friends and dependable.*
- *I am not haughty or cynical toward others.*
- *I try to live in a spirit of genuine honesty and truth.*
- *I do not restrict my love by barriers of race, social class or creed.*

- *I express my love especially in my service and generosity to the poor and the powerless.*
- *I try genuinely to listen to others.*
- *I am considerate of others and their property.*
- *my words and judgments are made in a spirit of kindness and charity.*
- *I easily pardon the weaknesses and sins of others against me.*
- *I am prompt to ask forgiveness when I have hurt or sinned against others.*
- *I go out of my way to help my neighbor.*
- *I am concerned for the effect of my actions and words upon others.*

When Christ freed us, he meant us to remain free. Therefore stand your ground, and do not submit again to a yoke of slavery (Gal. 5:1).

A Christian is free:

- *from the slavery of his passions, which he governs.*
- *from idols such as money, material comfort, power, luxury, and false forms of love.*
- *from the sin of self-love and egotism.*
- *from prejudice which narrows love and makes it unlike the love of God.*
- *from the need to defend and justify oneself constantly. He can admit his sins and failures, and he willingly accepts helpful criticism and advice.*
- *from falsehoods in his search for truth. He does not accept imposed answers, nor does*

he restrict himself to the opinions of any one "class."

My dear people, let us love one another, for love comes from God and everyone who loves is of God (1 John 4:7).

God's love is made visible in the sacrament of marriage. Therefore the Christian:

- *exhibits a healthy attitude toward sex as a gift of God and avoids the extremes of prudishness and licentiousness.*
- *avoids all love of the flesh for its own sake.*
- *accepts the vocation to marriage or to celibacy as a gift of God and finds in his particular vocation a means of drawing closer to God's love.*
- *is totally faithful to his spouse as a reflection of God's fidelity to his people.*

Christian love radiates outward into the family. The Christian:

- *honors his parents and shows them respect.*
- *is not ashamed of his parents or relatives because of some involuntary fault such as modest origins or foreign accent.*
- *is willing, when able, to return his parents' love by providing for them in old age and through other acts of tenderness and charity.*
- *is concerned to provide in his life a good example for his children to imitate.*
- *provides for his children through emotional, economic and educational security.*

Go into the entire world and proclaim the good news to all creation (Mark 16:16).

Every Christian has a mission to his fellow men. Therefore:

- *he supports the Church's work through his talents and money.*
- *he is not ashamed to reveal himself as a Christian and to give witness to his belief.*
- *he gives money and time to working for different charitable causes.*
- *he takes his political responsibilties seriously.*
- *he keeps informed on current events and votes intelligently.*

The Christian is mindful that he has been appointed the guardian over God's creation. Therefore:

- *he uses his environment without polluting it unnecessarily.*
- *he is careful in his use of material goods and avoids carelessness and excessive waste.*

The Christian recognizes his occupation as an excellent means to express his love of God. Therefore:

- *he does his job without laziness or carelessness.*
- *he is careful to acquire and maintain occupational and technical competence.*

Father, may they be one in us, as you are in me and I in you (John 17:21).

The Christian is called to make visible in the world the unity already present in God. Therefore:

- *he strives to overcome dissension and misunderstandings and to create in their place a spirit of peace and brotherhood.*
- *he begins the work of peace in his own life, in his work and in his family; then through his money and talents he extends that peace throughout the world.*
- *he opposes war vigorously and will only allow himself to fight in self-defense and when peaceful measures have been exhausted.*
- *he is eager through prayer and work to help heal the sinful divisions that hurt the unity of Christ's Church.*

There is a variety of gifts but always the same Spirit: there are varieties of service, but all are for the same Lord (1 Cor. 12:4).

The Christian serves God by:

- *letting the entire community benefit from his gifts and capabilities.*
- *developing to their fullest his own innate talents, cultivating his mind, and keeping his body healthy.*
- *using his talents in a spirit of humility and service, without either pride or boasting.*
- *refusing to limit his service to any specific group, be it parish, family or friends.*
- *showing respect and appreciation for the talents and gifts of others.*

- *being willing to work with and cooperate with others in group projects.*
- *avoiding an attitude of domination when in a position of authority or an attitude of rebelliousness when working under another.*

Brothers and sisters, you will always have trials, but when they come, treat them as a happy privilege—your faith is only put to the test to make you patient (James 1:2).

The Christian:

- *is patient with his own faults and those of others.*
- *never despairs since he knows that God's goodness and mercy will triumph and that he is loved by God in spite of his sins.*
- *bears hardship and suffering ungrudgingly, mindful of Jesus' suffering.*

"Lord, be merciful to me, a sinner!"

"Your sins are forgiven. Now go, my brother, and sin no more."

Part V
The Rituals of Christianity (continued)

11

Sacraments of Healing—
Reconciliation and Anointing

The symbolics of healing

Sacraments are not magic. They do not overwhelm with their power. And most Christians unfortunately often fail to live up to their call. The Church is holy and at the same time sinful—she is composed of men who have been given Christ's vision, baptized into his name and fed on his body, but yet allow strife, anger, envy, lust, and malice to dominate their life at times. When strife and sin appear in a human community, that society is hurt. If one member of a family injures another, the family suffers. If the injury is severe the family is torn, perhaps destroyed—divorce looms on the horizon. Similarly, a serious sin alienates a man from his fellow men: his relationships with others in that society are threatened or even terminated. He finds himself cut off—exiled from the group.

Jesus brought reconciliation. He calls men to come together and forgive each other. The family of man torn by wars, feuds, bitterness, harsh words and greed must be reunited in a fellowship of forgiveness and reconciliation. Jesus' ministry is one of healing.

Healing is a universal phenomenon and it is manifested among men under two symbols. The first is associated with physical healing. Oil was often used as a salve to apply to wounds to promote their healing. Even today we recognize certain medicinal properties in oil. It soothes the pain of burns; it can be used to clean a man; it restores health and vitality to dried skin and gives the person a youthful look.

The second symbol of healing lifts us out of the world into purely human experience. We have seen symbols so far as material parts of our earth: water, fire, oil, bread and wine. But forgiveness is a particularly human symbol of healing: it is not an artifact; we cannot place it before us on a table and inspect it. We want to say that it is spiritual rather than material.

But forgiveness has a very definite material aspect. For as a human reality it is as much a part of our bodily self as of some spiritual self. Forgiveness occurs after a split has taken place between people. Something has been done to upset or even destroy a relationship. A husband has let his anger flare out against his wife; good friends let envy for one another eat away at their friendship. When a relation is broken, if the breach is to be healed it must be done through the symbol of forgiveness.

And forgiveness always involves some bodily action, even if no more than saying the words, "I'm sorry," and hearing in response, "It's all right." Depending upon the culture and the people, forgiveness takes on almost an infinite variety of bodily forms all relating to the request of forgiveness and the granting of pardon. A husband brings home a bouquet of roses and his wife replies by a warm kiss. A child goes out of his way to do some chore, and the mother in turn offers a cookie as a token of her forgiveness.

No matter the form, forgiveness always involves something material, a word, a formula, an embrace, a tear. It also involves a personal interaction. The offender confesses he is wrong and asks for forgiveness. The wronged party accepts the request and forgives. The people are reconciled and the relationship restored.

Inconstant Israel

Inasmuch as Israel was a nation held together under the leadership of God, every sin and disruption of a man's relations with his neighbor threatened the fabric of Israel's society, and therefore man's relation to God. Every sin against one's neighbor was a sin against God inasmuch as God communicates to man through the nation and within the national and societal structures of Israel. There is no sin solely against God—all sin is social, against one's fellow man.

Israel's prophetic teaching was of a just God. God is righteous, holy, and abhors sin. In the eyes of Israel's prophets, Israel fell to the sword of her enemies because she refused to live in holiness and righteousness. Brother slew brother; man cheated and robbed his fellows; truthfulness was held of little value. The society degenerated; it became rotten and ripe for the conquest. God, being righteous, gave his people over to their just deserts.

But if God is just, he is also merciful, and the theme of his mercy appears also in the prophets.

He will bring down judgment upon Israel, but only so that she might come to her senses and return to him. She must return to the covenant God had made with her in which he showed how men must live together in peace and harmony. He is willing to forgive if only Israel will repent and ask forgiveness. And in the future the prophets see Israel re-established with a new covenant—a covenant written in men's hearts. The righteousness of God shall overcome and heal the divisiveness of man. As the prophet Isaiah saw, "Nation shall not lift sword against nation nor be trained for war."

The blind see, the lame walk!

That new day has come in the person of Jesus. An important part of Jesus' ministry was healing. He made the blind see, the lame walk—and this was one of the signs of the great day Isaiah and the prophets had foretold. He healed men's bodies and their spirits. A lame man was once brought to him to be cured. Jesus said to the man, "Your sins are forgiven." Immediately the scribes and Pharisees, men educated in the Jewish faith, were horrified. Any Jew knew that only God could forgive sins. Then Jesus turns to them and asks which is more difficult, to heal a lame man or to forgive sins. The theologically correct answer of course was the latter, but the old maxim says seeing is believing. "So that you may believe I have power to forgive men's sins I say to this man, get up and walk: your sins are forgiven." And the lame man walked, the Gospel reports.

The forgiveness of sins and the healing of man's physical infirmities were two important aspects of Jesus' ministry. So that his Church could carry on that ministry in his name, Jesus imparted to his disciples the power to heal spiritually and physically. The Acts of the Apostles depicts Peter and the other apostles carrying on this healing ministry.

At first the disciples understood this power to forgive sins primarily in terms of baptism. This sacrament washes a man clean from any sins he may have committed. And early Christianity demanded an exemplary moral and holy life from its converts. If a Christian fell into serious sin such as adultery, he was expelled from the Christian community.

In the first centuries four sins were thought worthy of excommunication (expulsion from the Church): murder, adultery, heresy (holding a theology that had been declared false) and apostasy (deserting or refusing to testify in public that one was a Christian). Men were cut off from the Church for such acts and it was questionable whether they could ever be readmitted. Eventually the Church decided that such sinners could be restored to union provided that they repented and did penance.

Around the eighth century Christians began seeking out monks (men who had retired from worldly life for a life of Christian perfection) for spiritual guidance. They confessed their faults to these monks and received pardon and a penance to perform. This custom grew into the present sacrament of reconciliation.

While the Church has not always practiced this sacrament as modern Catholics are familiar with it, she has always been aware that Jesus has put into her hands the power to forgive sins in his name. This assurance has remained constant, but how the Church has employed this power throughout the ages has changed considerably.

Be reconciled and healed!

In recent years the practice of confession has again undergone considerable change. Today it is possible for a Catholic to receive the sacrament in a number of ways. He may go into a church and confess his sins to a priest in a confessional (a small booth found in any Catholic church). Most Catholics in the past have received the sacrament this way. But one may also receive the sacrament in the priest's study or any other suitable place. In this way the sacrament can be a more relaxed and personal experience as opposed to the anonymity of the confessional. For confession, a Christian examines his life to assess how he is living up to his Christian vocation. He may want to discuss a problem with the priest or ask advice: all of this may be done within the context of the sacrament in the healing love of Jesus Christ.

Catholics today are also rediscovering the community dimensions of reconciliation. It cannot be emphasized enough that a Christian is first of all a member of a family, a society, a nation. Sin cuts him off from God *because* it has destroyed his relation to his neighbor. Reconciliation restores the sinner's relation to his fellow Christians at the same time that it restores him to unity with God.

Catholicism emphasizes the need to confess one's sins to a priest so greatly not because man cannot confess directly to God: he can and does. But his relation to God is as part of a people. God has become man and taken on a human body; he has chosen to work through human realities and human structures. He has become visible first in Jesus and today in our brothers, particularly our brother Christians. And he offers us reconciliation through men, representatives of his Church. Sin cuts us from the Church as much as from God. The sacrament of reconciliation through the person of the priest, representing the Church, receives the sinner back into communion.

This communal aspect of reconciliation is emphasized through special reconciliation services. Here Christians come together to pray, meditate and examine their lives. How have they been living up to the light they carry within them? Have they treated their brother as a brother? At a point within this service there is the opportunity to go to a priest and confess privately. Then the priests give absolution to the people together. Thus the community is healed, brought back together and washed clean again.

There is no absolute rule on the place of the sacrament of reconciliation in a Christian's life. It is necessary if he has sinned gravely: if he has destroyed or seriously wounded his relations with another man. Hopefully such a serious sin will be an infrequent occurrence. But if we do not often fall into serious sin, yet most of us fail to live up to our calling. Much of our life has not yet been transformed into Christ, and the sacrament of reconciliation used in a mature manner becomes a gifted moment when we can review our actions and thoughts in the light of the commission we received in confirmation. Acknowledging those areas in need of improvement, we receive Christ's healing power enabling us to continue to grow into his being. Reconciliation is the most personal of the sacraments: a meeting with the Lord who heals and reconciles. Too often in the past Catholics have thought of this sacrament in terms of being judged; its real value lies in hope and forgiveness.

Christ's ministry also involved the healing of physical maladies, and this ministry too was entrusted to his followers. Whenever a Christian is seriously ill a priest is called to administer the sacrament of anointing. The priest comes to the sick person and together with the family prays for a restoration of health. He then anoints the man with oil in Christ's name. Thus even sickness is transformed into a possibility of encountering the Lord. No magic is involved; the person does not infallibly recover. But faith has a healing power and through sickness and weakness the Christian might come closer to understanding Jesus and his vision and might even have his health restored by that vision, or if full recovery is impossible the patient might receive the strength to bear the illness and suffering in Christ's name.

Psalm 51 is one of Israel's great songs of lament for her sins.

John 11 recounts Jesus' raising of

Lazarus from the dead and shows his power over life.

Jesus passes on his authority to forgive sins to his disciples in John 20:19-29.

Peter carries on Jesus' healing ministry in Acts 3:1-10

James 5:12-20 indicates the presence of the ministries of reconciliation and healing in the apostolic Church

 The Church Praying

Penitential Rite from the Mass

Priest: *My brothers and sisters, to prepare our-selves to celebrate the sacred mysteries, let us call to mind our sins.*

All: *I confess to almighty God, and to you, my brothers and sisters, that I have sinned through my own fault in my thoughts and in my words, in what I have done, and what I have failed to do; and I ask blessed Mary, ever virgin, all the angels and saints, and you, my brothers and sisters, to pray for me to the Lord our God.*

Priest: *May almighty God have mercy on us, forgive us our sins, and bring us to everlasting life.*

People: *Amen.*

12

Sacraments of Christian Witness— Marriage and Priesthood

Sacrament of love—Christian marriage

All human societies practice some form of marriage—a more or less permanent relationship between a man and a woman. The dominant symbol of the relation is the act of sexual intercourse: the most powerful expression of man's desire to unite with another. Plato even suggested that originally men and women were joined together as one creature with four arms and legs. But they were separated into two creatures and ever since they have been striving to reunite with one another.

Sexual intercourse communicates human love. In intercourse the man and woman give themselves to one another. Such is not always the case, but we are speaking now of the exemplar rather than the rule. The total abandonment to the other person in the bodily fulfillment of sex mirrors on the physical plane the self-sacrifice to the beloved that true love requires. Sexual intercourse serves as a sign of the couple's love at the same time that it strengthens, deepens and promotes their love.

The prophets of Israel used the symbol of marriage to describe God. Yahweh was a bridegroom and Israel his bride. Seeing her in Egypt he had fallen in love. He chose her for his own, brought her out of Egypt, washed her clean in the Red Sea, and took her for his wife, to have and to hold forever.

But Israel had been unfaithful; she had played the whore. Chasing after other gods she forgot her marriage and what God had done for her. Again and again in the prophets God pleads with Israel to return, to honor her marriage. Hosea is commanded to illustrate Israel's situation painfully in his own life: he marries a prostitute who constantly deserts Hosea to run after other men. But again and again God asks Hosea to take her back and to forgive her adultery.

The tragic marriage of Yahweh and Israel should rightfully end in divorce. Israel frequently does not act the wife and bride. She deserts her bridegroom often, fickle to the core. But God on his part is faithful. He punishes Israel only to make her see her infidelity, only to coax her to return to her true home. Although he has more than enough cause, he will not give in to a divorce—Israel may abandon her home and lie with every idol she fancies. Yahweh still waits for her to return, ever ready to forgive her.

This symbol of marriage becomes one of the central metaphors of the Christian experience. Now however Christ is the bridegroom and the Church his bride. Jesus proves the extent to which God would go for his beloved—he gives up his life for her. Jesus cannot divorce his Church—he has given his promise and already made the ultimate sacrifice for her. Yahweh made marriage a relation of faith;

Jesus adds the dimension of permanence to the marriage symbol. The human symbol of marriage is enriched and given fuller meaning through Yahweh and Jesus. God's love for man speaks of a union between two persons; it is a love faithful in spite of infidelity, a love willing to sacrifice, a love constant and permanent.

The Christian couple through their marriage are called upon to manifest in their love for one another the love of Jesus for his Church. Christian marriage becomes a school of love. True deep love is not easily come by. Most people probably enter marriage merely infatuated with each other or merely in love with love itself. But love is unreal until it is enfleshed. In marriage's school we learn slowly and often painfully how really to love one another. We are selfish and we are used to thinking of ourselves first. But when we marry we are no longer alone; there are now two of us wanting to be one. And this unity can only be learned in love. We must learn sacrifice. Only then can we truly know love. John says that the greatest love a man has is to give up his life for another—this of course is Jesus' love and he is the master in the Christian school.

Marriage is raised to a Christian sacrament because it is a unique opportunity to encounter Jesus Christ. The God who is love can be experienced in the human institution of marriage. As the man and woman grow in love for one another they experience Jesus in a very real way. Christian love is not some unearthly idea, but the everyday love of one human being for another, and this love is focused in marriage.

The sacrament of marriage is not a once in a lifetime moment, present in the marriage ceremony.

The sacrament, the encounter with love, continues for the rest of our lives. In every expression of love Jesus is once again made flesh—given body. Christian marriage should extend Jesus' experience into every corner of human existence. Love radiates outward; it cannot be contained or bottled up: it demands to flow in giving. The love between husband and wife overflows in their love for their children, and if powerful enough it transforms their friends as well. The mission of Christian marriage does not speak of Christ's love: it *loves*. And love speaks louder than any words.

Inasmuch as Christian marriage is a growing in the love of Christ, an experience of the God who is love, it must also reflect the permanence of God's love. God did not forsake Israel and Christ will never divorce the Church. God's love is completely unconditional—he will not revoke it once it has been given. Jesus did not hesitate to live out to the end the consequences of his love—death on a cross.

Similarly a Christian marriage, if it is truly to participate in Christ's love, must involve total commitment, unconditioned by any reality other than death. Love can only exist and grow if there are no strings attached: I cannot really love you if I intend to quit loving should certain conditions not be fulfilled.

Love is not easily come by in our world—it is not similar to attraction or affection. It does not in the least depend upon some innate lovability in the person. No one is lovable until he is loved. A man and woman who marry do so committed to learn to love each other. Love cannot grow if they give up when the going becomes rough: only in the rough going can true love begin. Only in the rough going do we come to see our need for our beloved, our anguish in being alone: the truth that we were made for another and that we die unless united in love.

Sacrament of service—Christian priesthood

Jesus preached the centrality of love, and his actions taught that love finds fulfillment in service. This experience was entrusted to a select group of men, his disciples. These men were responsible for bringing the good news to the world. They serve God for the sake of men and men for the sake of God.

Priesthood is a structure found in all man's religions. The priest acts as a bridge between his fellow men and God. He is a mediator. He offers sacrifice to God in the name of his fellows; he oversees and performs the sacred ritual by which the religious experience is conveyed; he preserves and protects the religion from deformation and corruption. He pleads on behalf of the people to God: he asks for rain so that the crops might grow, prays over the sick for their recovery, asks for victory in battle. Because of his sacred duties he is a special person—holy, dedicated to the things of God.

Israel began to distinguish between the various functions of the priest. In her early days she too had a priestly office. But the prophets saw Israel itself as a priestly people. Israel stood before God; Israel received God's Word for men. Israel herself was different from the other nations—holy and dedicated to God.

When Israel was freed from her bondage in

Babylon and allowed to return to her land, her conception of her priesthood grows. The Isaiah of the exile sees Israel as a priestly people because she mediates God to men. And in the strange and beautiful "Songs of the Suffering Servant" Israel herself becomes a priestly sacrifice to God on behalf of the nations. God works through Israel for all men: Israel is the light of God meant to dispel every man's darkness.

But Israel never fully realized her priesthood for the nations. This strand in her self-concept never came into prominence. Not until Jesus does it burst into blossom. Very early Christians saw in Jesus the Suffering Servant, the one who takes upon himself all our burdens, divisions and sin. He offers himself to God on our behalf, and his life becomes a sacrifice through which man and God are brought together.

Jesus is the one true priest because he is the true mediator. Really man and really God, he forms the bridge between God and man: making the divine human and the human divine. He offered himself in sacrifice to God on the cross. Unlike Israel he was obedient to God even to his death. He fulfilled perfectly the old covenant with Israel. And because he completed it he himself became the new covenant. This new contract cannot be broken because it has already been perfectly fulfilled in Jesus. It does not depend upon our work but upon his work accomplished on the cross. We have but to incorporate ourselves into Jesus in order to enter into this new contract. We have but to believe in him to be saved.

Baptized into Christ's body we become part of

that body. As he was the priest of the world, so every Christian shares in his priesthood: the world encounters Christ through the Christian. The covenant sealed on the cross contains good news for every man—it contains man's freedom from condemnation and death, it unfolds the essence of reality: God's love. The Christian's priesthood brings this covenant to all men. For all must hear the good news that is theirs: the freedom and love they need not earn or labor for because it is given to them freely as a gift.

Such is the Christian's priesthood—to bring God to the world and the world to God. Christian priesthood is bestowed in baptism; in confirmation Christians are seated by the Holy Spirit and commissioned. They are reconcilers between man and God because man and God are *already fully* reconciled in Jesus Christ and man needs only to be brought to awareness of it.

The Christian community also needs special men to devote full-time service to the faith. At first Christians appointed men to be the disciples' helpers. Then teachers were needed to pass on the experience and the dogmas. Preachers were needed to proclaim God's eternal Word to men immersed in changing time. And ministers were needed to administer and oversee the sacramental aspects of Christian life.

Out of this practical necessity grew the cultic priesthood in the Church. This forms a special priesthood. These men devote their lives to the Church and the Christian people. They mediate in a certain way between God and his people inasmuch as they teach the faith, preach the Word and administer the Church's rituals and sacraments. They exist to serve the Christian priesthood that belongs to every Christian, not to supplant it. They do not intervene between man and God but serve as instruments through which Christ's continuing work on earth is channeled.

The ministerial priesthood does not only serve a purely practical function, however. Like marriage it is a sacrament of Christian witness. The priesthood is a symbol through which a facet of Christ's vision becomes enfleshed in the world. Christian marriage is a focus for Christ's love: Christian priesthood becomes a focus for Christ's service.

Jesus taught his disciples that priesthood is an office of service rather than glory. The day before he died, John relates, he went around the dinner table and washed the feet of his disciples. In this action he caught the essence of Christian priesthood. Christ's ministers are not meant to be served but to minister to others. Christian priests do not live for their own sakes but for the sake of God's people. The minister gives up his own life to follow the example of the one true priest who gave up his life on a cross.

The sacrament of priesthood offers a man the challenge to encounter Jesus through a life of service and ministry. Just as Christian marriage enfleshes for the couple Jesus the lover, so Christian priesthood enfleshes for the minister Jesus the servant of all men. As Jesus existed for other men before himself so the priest puts on Jesus by dying to his selfishness and living for his people.

But priesthood is also a sacrament to all men. The priest accepts the duty and mission to show

Christ the servant in his life. Assuming the office of
priest he assumes the obligation to make his life
transparent to Jesus. Men must be able to see Jesus
the servant concretely present in the life of his
priest. The priest strives to incarnate this aspect of
Jesus into the world just as the Christian couple
incarnates Christ's love. Both sacraments carry this
two-pronged significance: they allow the recipient
to discover Christ in everyday life, and they also
call the recipient to show forth Christ to the world
in love or service.

Unfortunately Christians have often failed to
realize these sacraments in their lives. Many Christian marriages do not proclaim love and are tor-
tured with hate and selfishness. Similarly some
Christian priests have sought power and glory for
themselves rather than service to others. Christ's
servant cannot wash his fellow man's feet in ermine
robes.

But the failure of Christians and their distortion
of the sacraments and of Christ's vision itself serves
more to manifest the power of that vision than its
weakness. How that vision could continue to il-
lumine men in spite of the great distortions it has
suffered through the centuries is a miracle. It is not
so surprising that there have been Christian sinners
but that in spite of their great abundance there have
still been Christian saints. That Jesus' vision has
not been lost or damaged through the sinfulness of
his followers, that it has undergone resurrection after
every crucifixion Christians have inflicted upon it,
is surely a testimony of its truth and its power to
prevail over our sinfulness and death. That an
organization as corrupt as the Church can still pro-

duce holy men may be a sign of its divinity. God was perverse to choose to come among us as a mortal man. He has compounded the daring by remaining among us and working through sinful men and in a sinful institution.

> *Marriage:*
> *Ezekiel uses the image of marriage to describe Israel in chapter 16. Hosea's story is in the first three chapters of his prophecy.*
> *Ephesians 5:21-33 compares the Church to the bride.*
>
> *Priesthood:*
> *The entire letter to the Hebrews develops the theology of Jesus' priesthood.*

 The Church Praying

From the Marriage Ceremony

Father, all-powerful and ever-living God,
we do well always and everywhere to give you thanks.

You created man in love to share your divine life.
We see his high destiny in the love of husband and wife,
which bears the imprint of your own divine love.

Love is man's origin,
love is his constant calling,
love is his fulfillment in heaven

The love of man and woman
is made holy in the sacrament of marriage,
and becomes the mirror of your everlasing love.

Lord, may all married couples praise you when they
*   are happy*
and turn to you in their sorrows.
May they be glad that you help them in their work
and know that you are with them in their need.
May they pray to you in the community of the
*   Church,*
and be your witnesses in the world.
May they reach old age in the company of their
*   friends,*
and come at last to the kingdom of heaven.
Amen.

Part VI
The Social Institutions
of Christianity

13

A Vision of a New Jerusalem

The politics of God

Whenever three or more men come together for any length of time a committee inevitably develops. We are social animals: we cannot live alone. To be human we need to live with other men, and our humanity, that which sets us above the animals, our thought and our language, arises out of our interaction. But if men are to live together some sort of structure is necessary. We quickly learn we are better off if each man does not proceed on his own. We are more successful if we hunt the animals together, if we grow our crops together, one man growing wheat, another potatoes, another apples. Some men are stronger and better able to defend the community. Some are better at getting along with people and are gifted with the art of governing.

As men group themselves into societies the structure of living becomes more complex and greater benefits become available than are possible in solitary existence. The social structure frees a man to exercise his particular talent and the society as a whole benefits.

Israel's God was a God of the nation, the human

society, not a God of separate individuals. Yahweh is my God and he is also your God, but more, he is our God. He brings diverse men together into a nation, a society. He then rules and guides through the political activities of kingship, prophecy and law. For Israel, unlike Egypt and Babylonia, man is a unique individual who must not be crushed in the mob but who can only become fully human and transcend toward the righteousness and holiness of God as a member of a society.

Yahweh is a God of politics and history. He is present in the marketplaces and battlefields of the world. He is not the abstract, intellectual God of the Greek philosophers: too pure to be involved in the transitoriness of human affairs. Yahweh does not shrink from dirtying his hands. And he finally immerses himself completely in the finite history of man. He becomes a man of flesh and blood, laughter and tears, energy and weakness.

Jesus differs not from Israel's God. The God who freed a group of slaves from Egypt and made them a nation, the God who abandoned that nation to conquest by the Babylonians, the Greeks, then the Romans, could be expected eventually to become inextricably involved in history. And he could do so only by becoming man.

Nor does God's involvement in history end with Jesus. There is no reversal to this un-God-like behavior. Through the incarnation God is irrevocably tied to our history—our daily living—the confusing, finite and intricate matrix of human affairs. The God become man in Jesus becomes a human society in Christ's Church. The God who took upon himself a human heart, brain, arms and legs, emotions and thoughts, has now taken upon himself all the structures of a human society.

Incredible to believe such an obviously human institution as the Church contains God on earth! But it is no more incredible than believing that a man shrieking in pain and suffering on a cross is God. The scandal of the Church is only the scandal of Jesus and the scandal of Israel continued. But as God's presence within history intensifies, the incredibility and the scandal increases.

Since the essence of Christianity is the experience and vision of Jesus, we can more easily understand why it should flow through a Church. Experience is only alive in people; it cannot be preserved in some book. The book you are reading now at best can only describe; it cannot give the full experience of Christianity: God works through man, he revealed his essence to us in a man, and we come to know him today through other men living in his vision and sharing his experience.

The bride and body of Christ

Just what is the Church, though? How have Christians understood themselves as a Church, a community of Jesus? Israel had seen herself as a nation dedicated to God. She was God's people on a pilgrimage through history, slowly wending her way toward history's end and the encounter with the God of history. Christians saw themselves as a continuation of Israel. The Church is the new Israel, the new people of God, who, although they continue the pilgrimage, yet have in Jesus the end of the pilgrimage already with them.

St. Paul develops two images of the Church in his letters. First the Church is the bride of Christ. Through the prophets God had spoken of his love for Israel: he had seen her in Egypt, had taken her to his heart and married her. Paul saw Jesus in a parallel relation to his Church: she is the new Israel, the bride he has ransomed by his cross and married forever.

But there is an even closer identification of Jesus and his Church in another Pauline image. The Christian community is Jesus' own body on earth today. All are members of this body which is led and governed by Christ, its head. All have various functions to perform, various talents to donate toward this body. Paul does not merely speak figuratively. In the truest sense of the word Christ is made flesh in the world today in the Church which confesses and believes in his name.

Steadfast faithfulness

Christians have Jesus' assurance that he is irrevocably committed to his Church. During his earthly ministry he chose the men whose duty it would be to carry his vision across the earth. He chose twelve men in particular and Peter to be their leader. To Peter he promised that come what may he would remain faithful to his Church, never abandoning her or divorcing her or allowing her to stray from him.

Christians gradually came to a deeper appreciation of this truth. When Christians talk of the infallibility of the Church they indicate Jesus' promise to stand by this community; he will not allow his people to fall away from him. His vision and experience will not die out or be lost in his community: until the end of time men will be able to come into contact with Jesus' experience, his victory, his outlook, through the Church founded on him. Inasmuch as Peter's successor in the Church's leadership, the pope, is the visible symbol of the community's unity and its continuity and identity with the original fellowship, the promise of infallibility rests in a special way with him. The pope becomes the abiding sign that Jesus' fidelity and protection rests with his Church.

Medieval pyramids

The stratification of society in the Middle Ages produced yet another image of the Church, this one basically hierarchical. Christians simply saw the Church in terms of her structure: a pyramid. The pope is the leader on top at the peak of the pyramid, then under him are the cardinals, then the bishops, then the priests, and finally, at the very bottom, the most numerous class, the people. This is a valid description of the Church's governmental structure, but it really does not approach the true nature of the Church. Imagine if the early Christians had based their understanding of Jesus on his physical appearance: he had long brown hair, brown eyes, was five feet eight inches tall and spoke with a Galilean accent. This nice description tells nothing really important about Jesus. It does not say who he is or why we follow him or what he offered to man. In the same way the pyramid image of the Church is inadequate because it says nothing truly significant. And many people were misled by the image: they thought that the pope was the essence of the Church, or perhaps the pope and the bishops, whereas in truth the essence of the Church resides in all Christians together. Today happily this pyramidal understanding is falling into obsolescence as a way of seeing the Church.

The handmaid of the Lord

Recently Christians have begun to see in Mary, the Lord's mother, an image of the Church. Originally Mary's role helped come to an understanding of Jesus, but the recent shift in emphasis sheds much light on the Church. Pope Paul VI encouraged this development when at the end of the Second Vatican Council he proclaimed Mary the Mother of the Church.

During the first centuries Mary came to be recognized as the Mother of God. By this title the early Christians affirmed her motherhood of the whole Jesus, both his divinity and his humanity. Such a confession prevented a splitting of Jesus' personality—his divinity and humanity were indissolubly fused together. If Mary is the Mother of God because she brought the Savior into this world, then the Church can see herself as the Mother of God also, for Christ continues throughout the ages to enter the world through the Church. In her eucharist, her preaching, her mission and her witness the Church truly makes Jesus flesh in the world.

Mary was the culmination and flower of Israel, totally open and receptive toward God. Because of her role as Jesus' mother she was preserved by God free from sin throughout her life. When contemplating Mary's holiness and sinlessness the Church must see herself also as the handmaid of the Lord. For in spite of the sinful and disobedient members that make her up, she is the body and bride of Christ and she is holy and sinless because he is holy and sinless. Like Mary we as the Church are not made so because of ourselves but because we stand in Jesus who does make us so.

Finally a long Christian tradition says that Mary after her life on earth ended was taken immediately up into heaven. This tradition, just as the traditions of Israel and Jesus, is not a literal description of an event but rather a conveyer of truth concerning God, an experience of God. In the story of Mary's assumption i.e., her complete fulfillment in God, Christians see the conclusion of God's work in the world. At the end all creation will be drawn toward God and transformed in his light. In Mary's assumption the Church sees her own destiny and goal: she will not be abandoned but will be drawn up into union with God. The victory already won by Christ's cross will eventually penetrate and transform the entire universe.

As members of Christ's Church we are not what we once were. Once we were men separated from our brothers in strife and division, sin and darkness. But now we are one because of Jesus.

We still act sinfully though we have been freed from sin: we still die though death is dead. But as we, the people of God, march through history, we are called to make the vision penetrate more and more into the world of man. The seed of that vision takes root in our life and from us it is sown further afield until the whole creation has been transformed and becomes in act what it already is in deed in Jesus Christ.

1 Peter 2:4-10 speaks of Christians as God's priestly people.

Paul sees the Church as Christ's bride in Ephesians 5:21-33 and as Christ's body in 1 Corinthians 12:4-30.

The Petrine promise is found in Matthew 16:13-20 and also in John 21.

Luke sees Mary as the epitome of Israel in Luke 1:26-38. 46-56 and John sees her as the figure of the Church at the beginning of Jesus' ministry (John 2:1-12) and at the cross at the end of the ministry (John 19:25-27). The woman in Revelation 12:1-17 is also a figure of the Church and of Mary.

14

The Civics of Incarnation

The flesh of permanence

Having seen how Christ works through his Church and how the Church sees herself, we now turn to the much more prosaic matter of Church organization. What is the machinery that keeps this institution running from day to day, from year to year? And first we must distinguish between the essential structures of the Church and the inessential, temporary and changeable elements. The former were given by Jesus himself in the early Church while the latter grew up as the result of some need during the course of the Church's life and could be replaced if they cease to serve a useful purpose.

Jesus' ministry was to the people of Israel, but a large proportion of his time was spent with a small group of men, twelve in all: his disciples. After his resurrection this group was sent to bring his vision to the rest of mankind. They were the authentic hand-picked transmitters of the Christian experience. From among the twelve Jesus chose Peter as leader: his office provided a center of unity for the disciples. He was not appointed a dictator or a monarch or a king but a leader. His office was not of power but of service.

Catholics believe the office of the disciples passed on to their successors called bishops. These men are not equal to the apostles; still they are the leaders of the community which the disciples established. In Greek the word "episcopos" means overseer: the bishop is the leader and teacher of a certain community of Christians. In the bishop resides the fullness of the priesthood: he celebrates all the sacraments with his people.

The office of Peter as the head of the disciples also passed to a successor now called the pope. The pope is a symbol of Christian unity and continuity: he is a sign of the Church's oneness both in time and space. The bishops and the pope govern Christ's Church. They are not the head of the Church: that is Jesus himself. They are the caretakers of the Christian community upon earth. They are symbols of Jesus in the world: they must teach and live his vision of service to their fellow men.

The bishop is the leader of a diocese and he is the head of the Catholic communities in that area. To his people he is a symbol of Jesus. One of his signs of office is a shepherd's crook, for just as Jesus called himself the good shepherd sent to care for the sheep, so the bishop cares for the Christian people, Christ's flock, in the name of Jesus. He is the teacher of the Christian experience, he celebrates with his people the sacraments, and he governs the affairs and charities of his diocese.

During the history of the Church at different times all of the bishops have come together in council to deliberate how the Church should respond to the pressing problems of the age. When they are in council together with the pope they form the highest legislative and teaching body of the Church.

Priests are helpers of the bishop and participate in his priesthood. (This is the reason the bishop ordains priests. Only the bishop holds the full powers of priesthood.) They work under him, helping to care for the needs of the Christian communities of his diocese. They preach the Word of God, teach the Christian experience, baptize, celebrate the eucharist, hear confessions, witness Christian marriages, anoint the sick and preside at Christian funerals. They see to the needs of individuals in their particular community called a parish. The parish priest is the Christian minister most individuals have contact with: he is their local leader and minister.

The third minister of the Church is the deacon. The deacon helps the priest by preaching the Word of God, baptizing, distributing communion, witnessing marriage and presiding at burials. This office fell into disuse during the past but today it is again revived because of the need for more ministers.

The changeable clothing of custom

The three offices of priesthood—bishop, priest, deacon—are the Christ-instituted ministries of service for the Christian community. But during the centuries other positions and organizations grew up within the Church to meet various needs. We can only mention a few in passing.

The pope has the privilege of appointing men to be cardinals. The office of cardinal is simply an honorary post within the Church. Any Christian may be honored by the office, although in fact cardinals today are taken from the body of bishops. Cardinals have only one official duty: they help elect the pope.

There are groups of men and women in the Church who are called religious. Gathered together into different communities they exist either because of a special work or mission or because of a special way of life. For example the Paulists are American priests working to mediate between American society and the Christian experience.

There are also communities of men known as brothers and of women known as sisters or nuns. These groups do special work such as teaching or nursing, and the members live together a life of special Christian witness. They take three vows of chastity, poverty and obedience as a special way of following Christ.

The Church exists to embrace all varieties and cultures of men and women and there are an almost infinite variety of life styles open to the Christian. It is not that one is better than the other. Each Christian has a unique life, a unique story to tell: some may be called to serve the Church as bishop, others as a sister, others as a doctor or a housewife. The only important thing is that whatever the vocation, it is lived in the light of the Savior. Every Christian life is holy and sacred to the extent that Jesus can be seen in it.

The office of bishop is developed in 1 Timothy 3:1-7.

The deacon is mentioned in Acts 6:1-7 and 1 Timothy 3:8-13.

The priests of the community are referred to in 1 Timothy 5:17-25 and in Titus 1:5-9.

Part VII
The Experience of
Christianity

15

Christian Faith:
The Experience of Prayer

Paul once described Christian existence as a life of faith, hope and love. We can do no better than follow Paul as we discuss three central facets of Christian experience. We have already focused upon Christian experience throughout our investigation, for Christianity is an experience and its stories, dogmas, rituals, ethics and social institutions are only the means by which we come into the presence of the experience and enter it. But faith, hope and love focus in a special way upon the experience of Christianity.

To walk in faith

As a man of faith the Christian believes in something: he holds something valuable and sacred. If need be he is willing to die for this faith, this belief. He is a committed man, with certain opinions and values. Meaning shapes his life. He does not drift; he has a goal and a purpose.

The Christian's faith is not in himself or another man or in nature or some impersonal force, but in a living and personal God. Only God gives meaning and purpose to life. Christians differ little from other men: they are not, as a lot, starry idealists or naive supernaturalists. For the most part they are a rather earthy lot. They live much as most people live, looking no further than necessary to find meaning. The clock stops ticking not because of God but because it needs to be wound. The sun rises not because God makes it come up but because the earth rotates. But behind the life of ordinary meaning there is a faith that we are not alone, that we are not in the unfeeling hands of an impersonal fate which cares not at all about us. Human and scientific meaning can be pushed only so far. Eventually we are confronted with an ultimate question. Is there any meaning outside of man and his fertile mind. Are we the only intelligence in the universe? Is love just a human consolation, a sentimental curse on a weak animal species? When a Christian pushes meaning to its outmost limit, he acknowledges in the end God.

No abstract God, the Christian God is concrete in the extreme. He is so individual he dared to take upon himself a human nature and to walk the earth at one point in time. No silent God, he speaks his Word into the universe and gives it meaning. He wishes to talk with man, to converse with him, enter into a personal relation with him. And Jesus' ministry taught us how to converse meaningfully with God, how to pray.

The man of faith is a man of prayer. He opens his inmost being to God, his most secret hopes, fears, desires and thoughts. A Christian cannot stand off, remaining on impersonal terms with God. He desires a union with God as close as that of a father and his son. He keeps nothing back; he gives himself freely in this dialogue, approaching his God with all his faults and his perfections, his weaknesses and his strengths.

Our Father in heaven

Christian prayer finds its perfection in the prayer Jesus gave his disciples, the Lord's prayer. This is the model for every Christian prayer to imitate. It begins with an address to God as our Father. God's fatherhood formed one of the central themes of Jesus' teaching. God is a Father to us and we should approach him accordingly. Naturally as a Father he is due our respect and reverence. But he is not forbidding or overly awesome either. Jesus elsewhere calls God "Abba" which means "Daddy": a term of endearment and intimacy. We need not be pretentious, we need not put on airs or a false formality. We need conceal no part of ourselves from him: we can be truly ourselves. God fully accepts us since he is Father.

Holy be your name

As our Father he is deserving of our praise and admiration, for he created all things. More powerful than anything we can imagine, he is beyond our every conception. He is mysterious and awesome as a father is to a small child. Because of the beauty of his creation, because of his love and care for us, we want to honor him, to praise him, to glorify him: holy be your name!

Your kingdom come

God promised to establish a kingdom, a nation of men joined together because of their union in God. Jesus came preaching the coming of God's kingdom. An ironic cut at the Christian religion is that Jesus came to bring a kingdom and the Church is what he got. The Church is not the kingdom, but the beginning of and the highway to the kingdom. We trust in the future kingdom of God because we have a foretaste in Christ's Church. The Christian believes in the kingdom and gives his life over to helping bring about the progressive realization of the kingdom on earth.

Christian faith looks toward the future. Great things have already happened in Christ, but now we must look forward to the fulfillment when the whole universe will be taken up into Jesus and presented to God as his kingdom. The kingdom is a vision and a goal, but through our efforts we can begin to build it not in daydreams but in human lives. Christian faith is optimistic: although alone man will fail and disappoint, still man in union with God can progress.

Your will be done, on earth as in heaven

In his will is our peace—not because God is anything like a tyrant or a dictator, but because his will accords with the nature of the universe. To follow his will means to be in harmony with man and creation. In his will lies the secret of our happiness.

The kingdom is realized through obedience to God's will. It is already here on earth in Jesus Christ through his total fidelity to God. In faithful obedience we do not lose our liberty and freedom. Rather only in the will of God can we achieve the freedom we were born for. We were born to love and be loved, to dwell in peace. And peace is ours only if men put off their selfishness and pride for the selflessness and humility seen in Jesus. We were born for beauty not ugliness, for harmony not discord. And to create harmony any composer will say that all the voices must follow a higher vision than their own individual melody. The individual strand of melody is not lost but blends into the greater beauty of the whole.

The kingdom implies a harmony among men, achieved only if all follow the will of a higher power. In his will is not only our harmony and our peace, but life itself. In the beginning, said the Israelites, God created the world out of chaos. Into confusion he brought order and harmony. John says the Light which is God entered the darkness and shone in the darkness. Creation is not over; God is still creating today. Into the chaos and confusion of human beings he brings order and harmony. Amid the destruction and wars of nations he is building a kingdom of peace. In our darkness a light has pierced whose name is Jesus. In the light may we do his will.

Give us today our daily bread

It is fine to honor God and to pray for such ideal and abstract realities as his kingdom, but many of us feel just a little too sophisticated to pray for our daily bread. We are twentieth-century men, far removed from the superstition that saw behind every happening the finger of God. God may have created the universe but he is not directly responsible for the thunderstorm which threatens me with its lightning. Why should I pray that he protect me?

Yet God did not shrink from being born a man; he has entered into the very real and particular world we inhabit. Our daily bread *is* his concern. Through such simple requests a Christian comes to know God and his will. We are like children who must grow up by continually asking questions: "Can I do this? May I have this apple?" If a child did not ask questions he could never grow into adulthood.

Our childish prayers to God are a school in Christian adulthood. They provide the opportunity to know God and ourselves as well by speaking to him of our deepest concerns. The way in which these prayers are answered shows us how God's will is taking shape in our lives. From infancy to adulthood, whether physically or spiritually, is a hard, long process.

God is no refuge when all else fails. We learn his will and his peace day by day. And we grow by the common bread he feeds us. But our daily bread is not only the mundane course of our lives: it is also the daily bread of the eucharist. For here our true daily bread is found: the bread which nourishes us and makes us grow in the knowledge and love of God. In God's Word heard there and in the example of Jesus played out there daily we discern God's will in our life. This eucharistic prayer which is Jesus himself is the center of Christian faith.

Forgive us our sins as we forgive those who sin against us

The kingdom is built upon forgiveness. Forgiving sins was a prominent aspect of Jesus' ministry and it continues as a highly visible characteristic of his community. God's kingdom is not approached through revenge or retaliation but through forgiveness and reconciliation. Harmony in the Church is not won without dissonance: the kingdom is built not by saints alone but by sinners who may become saints, nor can it survive unless it is humbly forgiving.

Our model again is Jesus who said that if someone should slap you on the face the only response is to turn the other cheek. Christians believe this to be so even though they often fail to live up to it. Our faith is in a God great enough to forgive any wrong. If we would be like him we too must have faith in the power of good over evil, in the victory of charity over vengeance. Retaliation destroys itself. The only way out of the vicious circle of sin and wrong is complete forgiveness. In Jesus all of us have been forgiven by God; can we not now forgive one another?

Do not bring us to the test but deliver us from evil

Our faith is not knowledge but trust and love. Its opposite is not unbelief but despair. Faith is not a philosophy; it is a way of living, an approach to reality. It is not something to be proved: it can only be seen and acknowledged. It cannot be stored up, but must be lived day by day. It has no magic charm to ward off evil. We are still human beings and fall to temptation, the temptation to be selfish, to hold grudges, to look out only for ourselves.

We can be certain of God's love and forgiveness but we can never be certain of ourselves. So we pray not to be put to the test. We have a great treasure in our keeping, and we must live in fear and trembling lest we dishonor it. Luther once cautioned: pray as if all depended on God and work as if all depends on yourself. Although the victory has been won, as long as we are on earth we live mostly on this side of the cross; Easter still lies on the other side.

Luke and John are the masters of prayer. Significant passages in Luke are 1:67-79; 11:1-13; 22:39-46.

The final discourse of Jesus and his prayer are found in John 14—17. This sums up John's whole theology.

1 Timothy 2:1-8 shows the importance of prayer in the early communities.

  The Church Praying

Important Christian Prayers

The Lord's Prayer

> *Our Father,*
> *who art in heaven,*
> *hallowed be thy name.*
> *Thy kingdom come,*
> *thy will be done*
>   *on earth as it is in heaven.*
> *Give us this day our daily bread*
> *and forgive us our trespasses*
>   *as we forgive those who trespass against us.*
> *And lead us not into temptation,*
>   *but deliver us from evil.*
>
>   *Amen.*

The Angel's Salutation

> *Hail Mary, full of grace,*
> *the Lord is with thee,*
> *Blessed art thou among women*
>   *and blessed is the fruit of thy womb, Jesus.*
> *Holy Mary, Mother of God,*

pray for us sinners now
and at the hour of our death.

Amen.

The Doxology

Glory be to the Father,
and to the Son,
and to the Holy Spirit.
As it was in the beginning,
is now, and ever shall be:
world without end.

Amen.

16

Christian Hope:
The Experience of the Future

Repent and believe!

The Christian faces toward the future. Jesus'
message was of a coming kingdom rather than
something already present. The kingdom is here but
it is also still yet to come. The earliest Christians
believed that Jesus would soon return to inaugurate
the kingdom, and they eagerly awaited this second
coming; for their age was one of crisis and apocalyptic. The present life for most was one of hardship
and suffering. They looked forward to the end of
the present era and the dawn of a new age when
God would put conditions right.

These Christians were a people of hope: for the
return of Jesus and the transformation of the world.
They hope for an end to their present suffering, for
the speedy consummation and fulfillment of history.
They envision Jesus coming on the clouds as a great
judge. Men would be brought before him and
would be judged as to whether they had walked in
the light or the darkness.

But this hope was not fulfilled. Perhaps they had
misunderstood Jesus. Perhaps the end is not so
imminent, and they will die before it comes. Al-

ready in the New Testament Paul corrected some of his communities for placing undue emphasis upon the time of the end. Christians slowly began to realize that the interim period might be longer than a few lifetimes. If Christianity were to survive until this postponed end it would have to rethink its place in the world.

If Jesus will come to bring the world to its completion within a few years, such things as Church structure or a Christian's relations with the secular world are of little concern. But if this community may last for a considerable time, then one begins to think about organization and working out a *modus vivendi* with the world. Had Christianity not done this it would have died out; that it did reorganize and rethink its vision was a sign and proof of its great vitality and spirit. From a religion primarily concerned with making men ready for the judgment day, it became a religion concerned to spread to the ends of the earth Jesus' vision in terms of life in this world. Very early Christians stopped hoping and waiting for the end to come and turned themselves toward the task of making Jesus enfleshed in the world.

Maybe another day

The last day was postponed, made more distant and individual. Rather than an occurrence rushing upon them, Christians saw the last day as a far-off point in history or, better, as the moment of their own death. As they meditated upon the end an elaborate series of images and concepts grew up: images of a final day of judgment, of the tortures of hell, of golden streets and angels' wings in heaven, of a place of purification for those not sufficiently holy to enter heaven immediately. This whole imaginative structure grows throughout the Middle Ages until it flowers in *The Divine Comedy* of Dante and *Paradise Lost* of Milton.

Today most Christians find it difficult to believe in places such as heaven, hell and purgatory because of the very concrete images which originally grew up in order to make these realities more credible to earlier Christians. But just as the Christian hope did not die out in earliest Christianity but was transformed into the vivid medieval images, so today the Christian hope is not dying but is once more being transposed.

Christians believe and hope in eternal life. Death is not the end. We believe in a man who conquered death and gives us eternal life. Today however we are more sophisticated and the concrete images of the afterlife such as flames and harps do not help our hope. We have a hope in the eventual triumph of God through Jesus over sin and evil. We have a hope that creation will end in peace and union rather than chaos and destruction. We have the hope that at death we shall be fulfilled rather than annihilated. The feeble love we have managed to ignite in this life will burst into flame, and our flame will be joined with all other men in the one fire of Jesus Christ.

Death, where is thy sting?

To understand Christian hope we must examine the many Christian symbols which have grown up around it. Christians do not take these signs literally. If one went up in a rocket ship one would not arrive at heaven's gate. Rather the Christian symbolic language of hope is a way of speaking, feeble though it is, about things beyond our imagination and ability to comprehend. Images and concepts of heaven, hell and judgment are vivid ways of pointing toward a truth and a hope: they are not maps of any territory.

There is one earthly end for us all: death. There is no way of avoiding it: it is the lot man was born to. Each society comes to a certain understanding of death, and it learns to cope with death in certain ways. It seems as though contemporary American society denies the reality of death. Think how often we use euphemisms to avoid confronting death head on: "he passed away" rather than "he died" is only the most obvious example. How the very word "cancer" sends a shudder through our society! For cancer inevitably means death. Instead of "corpse" or "body" we refer to the "loved one" and the room where the body is displayed is the "slumber room" as though it were not dead at all. Men only joke about those matters they take most seriously; today we have an abundance of sexual or religious jokes but how many stories of death are there? America is afraid to confront this very present reality. We are unwilling to "bury" our dead; instead we provide them with "perpetual care."

Nothing could be farther from an authentic Christian attitude toward death. For the early Christians death was a fact to be faced, but it held little true terror. For these men had already died in baptism and had risen to eternal life. Physical death was merely the final stripping away of what was earthly, the final bursting forth into the light.

Before the judgment seat

As the expectation of the world's end receded farther into the distance Christians began to think of their own individual death in terms of this last day. In my own death I pass over into eternity and encounter my Lord. The judgment of men is moved from the end of time to the end of each man's time.

But why should there be any idea of judgment? Is not the Christian experience that men are already justified? While this is perfectly true there is still the importance of history and the problem of human freedom to be accounted for.

Both Israel and Christianity experience God becoming most real to men in their history. Christianity cannot deny or denigrate history, for there salvation is worked out. Because man's deliverance from sin and death was accomplished upon the cross does not mean that it is unimportant what happens now. The victory won on the cross must penetrate into the entire fabric of history so that all of creation may be transformed and saved.

The Christian is not absolved from the task of history. He must appropriate the reality of his deliverance into his own life. To a Hebrew to know the truth was equivalent to doing the truth. A Jew knew God not if he intellectually acknowledged God's existence. Rather he knew God only if he was obedient to God in his life. Similarly, although we are rescued totally by Christ, still it is our mission to let Christ leaven our life. To be saved is not just a fact, it is a truth to be lived.

Christians take life seriously because in human lives and history God works. Our life shows the measure of our assimilation to Jesus' vision. As a man acts, so does he truly believe; if we believe the world is built on a loving God so we must act.

Although we are saved we live our lives in fear and trembling because of our great commission. And our death is the climax of our life: what we are then sums up our entire existence. From death we pass into the light of God. In his light our faults and failures will be shown up. We will show our belief by the story we have told. "Have you done the truth?" Such is the question awaiting every man.

Obviously most of us are guilty. We are lukewarm rather than on fire with the vision. Our lives have not been transparent to Jesus; at best we have been like smoked glass. Are we to be lost? Should we live in Christian fear rather than Christian hope?

The geography of eternity

In the days of persecution it was fairly easy either to be a Christian or to fall away. And the communities had to decide how to deal with those who denied the faith under pressure. Should the Church be just or should she be merciful? It was a momentous and extremely important decision. For it would determine whether Jesus' vision was for all men or for the few strong enough to incarnate it into their lives.

The decision fell in favor of mercy. Men who had failed were to be forgiven and received back into fellowship. But as the Church grew into a community containing many who were only nominal Christians, again the problem arose. But this time it arose concerning the final judgment. Would only the saints be united with God?

The earliest concepts of the next world pictured Jesus as judge, welcoming the good into heaven and condemning the evil to hell. But what of those men who were not great lights of virtue but not out and out villains either? Slowly the idea of a middle state arose. Those not yet ready to enter heaven went to a place of purgation where they were purified of the sluggishness toward God manifested on earth.

This doctrine of purgatory shows the concern of the Church to preserve the original Christian vision of God's mercy and forgiveness. If we are not good enough for heaven we need not be condemned to hell. Nor need we debase heaven's perfection and holiness by allowing sinful men a place there.

The experience of God's mercy is so overwhelming in Christianity that when during the Middle Ages Christ took on the primary characteristic of the judge on the Last Day, the Christian people through the figure of Mary preserved the experience of God's superabundant mercy. They felt that although Christ might condemn, yet Mary need never condemn and could plead with her son for the sinner.

Today the medieval over-emphasis upon Christ's judgment has been tempered by his mercy and the figure of Mary as the never-condemning pleader on our behalf can recede into the background. But that the Church should at one time have developed such a prominent role for Mary demonstrates the indomitable prominence of mercy and forgiveness within the Christian experience. Ours is to hope rather than to fear.

Unfortunately purgatory soon came to be understood quite literally. Originally none of the concepts of heaven, hell or purgatory were meant to be understood literally. They were not actual places; they merely represented relations to God.

Hell was the state that guaranteed man's freedom. For if every man were saved in spite of himself would he be free? Although God wishes to save everyone and draw him to himself, yet he will not violate man's freedom. Love may not be coercive. Man must be left the option to reject God. That state of closedness toward God is hell, and it is a Christian value judgment to call such a state hell. Christians say that the entirely self-sufficient man, the man who wills to live without love, is living in a state of hell. Fire and torture are merely images and are pale compared to the true pain a man inflicts upon himself through his selfishness.

Most men realize the value and need of love. Unfortunately in many ways they fail to live up to its demands in this life. They still have large areas of selfishness within them. They still grasp rather than give, whereas love is not love until it is given away. As these men grow in love they come closer to God. And their growth does not stop with death. For at death they will see God and the sight of God's love will burn away all of the selfishness and egotism remaining in us. The blinding and piercing sight of Love itself will wrench us away from our self-centeredness. We will be drawn unswervingly into the love which is life. Purgatory is no prison where most of us spend a sentenced amount of time. Purgatory is an image, like hell, to describe a way of life not only after death but this very minute. It should be the image of our life right now.

There are some men and women who have made their lives open to God; these are the saints, and at their death they join in full union with the object of their love. The state of this love is heaven. For most of us heaven is only a vision, a distant goal. Our life is a purgatory, not a heaven. But the idea of heaven shows us and keeps before us the hope that purgatory is only temporary. Heaven is everyone's final goal.

Heaven, hell and purgatory are three ways of living right now; they are three possibilities of human existence. Thus they are more than curious speculations concerning something we can never know this side of death. Our Christian life is lived in hope—a hope of heaven and a hope of God's infinite mercy. For his Church that would not expel sinners nor condemn men to hell hopes and lives in the faith that a God who loved man so much as to become a man in order to reach man will in the end again let his mercy triumph.

In the eucharist, the center of our Christian life, there is a real initiation of the Christian hope. In this sacrament God himself is offered to us in order to bring us into union. And he offers himself only on condition that we acknowledge our sinfulness and unworthiness. Before receiving the host we say,

"Lord, I am not worthy to receive you, but only say the word and I shall be healed." We do not need to be perfect; we can acknowledge our faults. And our confession is met not by a refusal but by the giving of God into communion with us. Here is a foretaste of our hope of fulfillment: here is the true image of our God.

Matthew 24 and 25 gives Jesus' discourse concerning the second coming and the Christian's attitude toward it.

Paul talks to his community at Thessalonica about the return of Jesus in 1 Thessalonians 4:1—5:11 and in 2 Thessalonians 1:1—3:5.

The final consolation of the Church is seen in the beautiful description of the heavenly Jerusalem in Revelation 21.

 The Church Praying

From the Service of Christian Burial

Father, all-powerful and ever living God,
we do well always and everywhere to give you thanks
through Jesus Christ our Lord.

In him, who rose from the dead,
our hope of resurrection dawned.

*The sadness of death gives way
to the bright promise of immortality.
Lord, for your faithful people life is changed, not
    ended.
When the body of our earthly dwelling lies in death
we gain an everlasting dwelling place in heaven.*

*May we then go forward eagerly to meet the Lord,
and after our life on earth
be united with our brothers and sisters
where every tear will be wiped away.*

Amen.

17

Christian Love:
The Experience of God

God is love

Time and again we have found that Christian experience is an experience of God as love. But what is love? Love unfortunately has become sentimental and trite; it has been downgraded to mean no more than affection. Love is the substance of Hollywood films; it is not substantial enough to build a way of life upon. Christianity however says God is love; it does not say love is God. The Christian experience of God teaches us what love truly is; sentimental love does not teach about God.

Paul describes love in his first letter to the Corinthians. From him we can resurrect love from sentimentality. What is love? Love makes life possible. For without love I do not exist: I am empty, a shell with no substance. Any action I perform has meaning only in proportion to the love contained in it.

Love is the base and foundation of the human universe, the motivating principle, the ground of all reality. Man is only really man if he lives grounded in love. Everything else is secondary: faith, hope, good works, great accomplishments.

What is love? It is patient, kind, it does not envy. Love makes a man concerned for other men rather than himself. It decreases our egotism and our pride. Without love we will exalt ourselves; we will come to an overly high estimate of our importance. We think all is well if only we are well.

Love means a dying to selfishness. We are not righteous and good because of ourselves. If we can bear to look at ourselves objectively, we are full of faults. We should not be "quick to take offense" when rebuked because, being human, we probably deserve to be rebuked. We are righteous and good because of God's love for us which makes us so.

"Love keeps no score of wrongs." Love is forgiving rather than revengeful. It realizes and accepts our human frail condition. If things go wrong, if a friend slights me, if my wife fails to meet me downtown on time, naturally I grow angry because I have been treated ill, and naturally I know that I deserve better treatment. It is not just, and I shall take steps to correct this injustice against me.

But "let him without sin cast the first stone." Can I, an unjust man, in good conscience condemn injustice when my own injustice has been forgiven, totally and unconditionally, in Jesus Christ? What now can I do against the injustice committed toward me? Retaliate? Seek revenge? The justice and righteousness of Jesus retaliated against Peter's denial on Holy Thursday by seeking Peter out to forgive him and commission him to head the new community on Easter Sunday. Can we who stand in Christ do less? Love "does not gloat over other men's sins, but delights in the truth."

To be selfless, humble and forgiving is difficult—

even impossible, it seems. It is easier to hold a grudge, or even to be sentimentally forgiving, than it is to love responsibly. We can not toss off forgiveness with a quick, "Oh, it was nothing." Love is responsible; it must be serious. If our brother has wronged and hurt us, we can not play the stoic and pretend that he has not touched us. Love calls us to respond to the hurt by opening ourselves even more to him. To love someone we must give ourselves over to him, and it is very difficult to make oneself vulnerable a second time. But how else can we understand the counsel to turn the other cheek?

We have only Paul's assurance that "there is nothing love cannot face." Somehow in Christ we can find the strength to respond to hatred with love. Although love seems so fragile, so wispy, so delicate, yet in Jesus' commitment in love even to the acceptance of the cross we see that "there is no limit to its faith, its hope, its endurance."

Love revealed

Christian love is based upon the most concrete exemplar possible. God shows us what love is: he loved the world so much that he gave his only Son so that the world might be brought into union with God. And the Son's example of love was to the extent of laying down his life so that we might be able to have life.

The perfect model of love is the Godhead itself. Jesus taught that God is our Father and is best spoken of as Love. The proper response to the

Father's love is to do the Father's will. We can see this in ordinary life: to show his wife how much he loves her, the husband may take her on the vacation she has always wanted to go on. He says, "I love you enough to do gladly what you wish rather than what I might want." True love willingly sacrifices itself. Jesus' love for the Father involved such total obedience that he did not shy away from the torturous death of crucifixion.

In Jesus' resurrection the disciples came to experience Jesus himself as God. They saw him as the bridge between God and man. Jesus is the true approach to the Father, and Christian prayer has always been spoken to the Father through Christ our Lord.

But the love between the Son and the Father is so concrete, so real, so life-giving that it too can be understood only as a person. This love is so powerful that it too has a separate existence. It is the third person of God which Christians call the Holy Spirit. The Holy Spirit within us draws us into the very Godhead itself.

Love compells the lover to be open to others. True love never shuts out anyone or anything. Marital love grows through the addition of a child to the family. If real love exists between the parents, there can be no jealousy over the child. The love between the two naturally radiates outward to include others within the orbit of that love. The two lovers who exist only for each other and who cannot stand the intrusion of the world into their "love" are at best infatuated with one another, not in love.

The love between the Father and the Son which

takes personal form in the Holy Spirit is sent forth to bring the entire creation within the orbit of that Love. When we realize that the Holy Spirit is the core of the Godhead, we see the great dynamism of God. His very essence is to go continually out of himself, to create and bring the creation back into himself.

In baptism and confirmation Christians receive within themselves the very Holy Spirit of God. And the early Greek Fathers of the Church described the Christian's life as a divinization of man. As the Spirit comes to control and to permeate our life, we become more and more Godlike ourselves.

Oh happy fault!

The ancient Hebrews told a story of the first man and woman, Adam and Eve. God placed them within a Garden of Eden where grew everything needed for their life and well-being. But God forbade them to eat the fruit of one tree in the Garden —the tree of the knowledge of good and evil. One day a serpent approached the woman Eve and tempted her to eat the forbidden fruit. "God would not want you to eat that fruit because then you too would be a god," whispers the serpent into Eve's ear.

And Eve, tempted to become like God, did eat the fruit and persuaded her husband Adam to eat the fruit as well. Unfortunately they did not become like gods; they became like the men we know, men who do not live in any paradisical garden but rather amid the thorns and pain of human existence.

Originally God meant man to be fulfilled and to be happy as a creature of God in union with him. But man was free and he chose to try to be like God by being equal to and independent of God. This first pride became rooted in the very nature of man, so that as man he is compelled to exalt himself as a god. But because he is a man he ultimately fails miserably.

God could have abandoned man to his fate and his misery of unfulfilled pride, but he did not. Man in the beginning went against the creator's plan for creation; he disobeyed and brought failure upon himself. The new initiative must lie with God.

Of course God might have shown man the way back to the proper position of humanity, and we could say he did this through Israel's law. But if he were to rescue man truly, somehow God must surpass even himself. What if he should fulfill man's original sinful desire to be like the gods? What if in order to make man like God, God should dare to become man?

God's reply to man's free act of disobedience in Adam is seen in Jesus Christ. Jesus is the second Adam who does obey God. But he is more. In him we actually are drawn into God as equals. God became man so that man could become God. Had man not sinned he would have lived as God's favorite creature, and he would have lived happily under God. But man's sin has shown clearly the extent of God's love. In Jesus we have more than we had in Adam, for in Jesus we have given to us the Holy Spirit who truly makes us like God. In the light of Jesus we can truly consider the fall of Adam happy because it has let shine upon us the brightness of God's love. Our disobedience is responded to out of all measure by the gift of God in Jesus.

The Trinity

The Trinity is the essence of Christianity because in the Trinity we find love's true nature, for God, although he is one, is yet three persons. The Father, the Son and the Spirit are all one in that they are God, but they form a dynamic rather than a static unity. The essence of God and therefore the essence of Love is sharing in union. The Trinity will always remain a mystery for us. We humbly acknowledge three persons in the one God. We confess that God is Father, Son and Holy Spirit while at the same time we confess that there are not three Gods, only one.

The doctrine of the Trinity is no idle speculation. It has an intimate relation to the Christian life. For the Christian through Christ and in the Holy Spirit is drawn into the very center of God into union with the Father. If the Christian comes to experience the three-in-oneness of God, he also comes to see the tri-une-ness of love. Love unites into one what was before separate. In the love of Jesus men come to understand that they cannot live alone. They are called to join with one another in love which is the creative and life-giving Spirit of God ever going out to embrace all creation and returning into the union of the Father.

In Jesus Christ lies our true destiny. We began with a question of meaning and of purpose, and we have found that question satisfied. Our heart has searched and questioned and been restless until it found that for which it was made. Our search ends only when we come to the home we are seeking and embrace the Father who, while we have been seeking Him, has been ceaselessly searching for us.

> *God's love for us is seen in Luke's parables of the prodigal son (Luke 15:11-32) and the good samaritan who is a figure of Christ (Luke 10:29-37).*
>
> *Paul's hymn to love is in 1 Corinthians 13.*
>
> *But the master of God's love in the New Testament is St. John whose first letter should be read in its entirety.*

 The Church Praying

The Easter Hymn

Rejoice now, all you heavenly choirs of angels.
Rejoice, all creation around his throne
　　for this mighty King is victorious.
Sound, O trumpet, tell of our salvation.
Rejoice too, O earth: you are made brilliant by such
　　splendor.
　　Rejoice, for you have been illumined.
　　Darkness everywhere has been overcome by the
　　brightness of this everlasting King.
It is truly right and just that with all the ardor of

our hearts and minds we should proclaim with our voices the invisible Almighty Father and his only begotten Son, our Lord Jesus Christ, who paid the debt of Adam for us to his eternal Father, and with his precious blood washed away the penalty of original sin.

This is the night which restores to grace and unites in holiness those who believe in Christ, separating them from worldly vice and the darkness of sin.

This is the night on which Christ burst the bonds of death and victoriously arose from the grave. For life itself, without redemption, would be of no avail to us.

O wondrous condescension of your mercy towards us!

How far beyond our understanding is your loving affection, that you would ransom a slave at the price of your Son.

O necessary sin of Adam, which was blotted out by the death of Christ.

O happy fault, that merited such a redeemer.

O truly blessed night which alone deserved to know the time and the hour when Christ arose from the grave.

The holiness of this night banishes wickedness and washes away sin and restores innocence to those who have fallen.

It puts hatred to flight, brings peace and humbles pride.

It is of this night that Scripture says:
"And the night shall be as bright as day.
And the night shall light up my joy."